Footprint Handbook

Cartagena & Caribbean Colombia

ANNA MARIA ESPSÄTER & BEN BOX

This is
Cartagena &
Caribbean
Colombia

Reaching Colombia's Caribbean coast is like entering another world. Steamy, colourful and lively, the entire area pulses to the seductive rhythms of *vallenato*, heard at festivals throughout the region.

Costeños may be looked down on by their more sombre countrymen, but they certainly know how to enjoy themselves. The Barranquilla Carnival is second only to Rio for colour and size, and is far less commercial. There is fine architecture and an impressive literary legacy here too, particularly in Cartagena, the emerald in the crown of Colombia. This stunning colonial city is positively bursting with colour and history, and offers fine food, a lively nightlife and various sparkling coral islands within easy reach.

South from Cartagena is Mompós, a colonial town with one of the best Easter festivals in the world. Around the Gulf of Urabá, on the way to Panama, is a wild shoreline of coral reefs backed by the virgin jungles of the Darién. Travel east and you'll reach Santa Marta, Colombia's oldest city and gateway to the spectacular Tayrona National Park. The Sierra Nevada de Santa Marta is the highest coastal mountain range in the world, with tropical beaches and snow-capped mountains within 20 miles of each other. It also conceals the Ciudad Perdida, the culmination of an unforgettable trek. Further east is the arid landscape of the Guajira Peninsula, home to the indigenous Wayúu and enormous flocks of flamingos, where turquoise waters lap against a desert shoreline.

Anna Maria Espsäter   Ben Box

Best of
Cartagena &
Caribbean
Colombia

top things to do and see

❶ Cartagena

Amble through the streets of the old town of Cartagena, where most of the colonial treasures can be easily visited on foot. Walk the ramparts for good views of the old Spanish buildings and the sea surrounding the city, then watch the sun set over the bay with a sundowner. Page 26.

❷ Islas del Rosario and San Bernardo

Soak up the sun, sea and sand on these quintessential Caribbean islands, part of Colombia's extensive network of national parks. Expect white-sand beaches, beautiful coral reefs and a laid-back vibe. Stay overnight for the full experience, away from the day-trippers. Pages 38 and 59.

❸ Mompós

Explore this beautifully preserved riverside town, a UNESCO World Heritage Site. It's well known for its extraordinary Easter celebrations and for Simón Bolívar's most important victory during the fight for Independence from the Spanish. The riverside location is also great for birdwatching. Page 54.

❹ Arboletes

Wallow in a mud bath the size of a swimming pool. The Volcán de Lodo, some 15 minutes from Arboletes, is the largest mud volcano in the area, only a stone's throw from the sea, allowing for a swift post-mud bath wash. Page 59.

Caribbean Sea

Puerto
Bolívar **7**
Manaure
Cabo de
la Vela Península de
la Guajira
Uribia
Riohacha
Maicao
5
PN Tayrona
Santa Marta Palomino
Ciudad Perdida **6**
Barranquilla *SFF Ciénaga*
Grande de ◆ *PNN Sierra*
Baranoa *Santa Marta* *Nevada*
Aracataca
Cartagena **1** Sabanalarga Fundación
Islas del Rosario Turbaco Malagana Valledupar
2 Malagana Bosconia
Islas de San Jacinto
San Bernardo Ovejas
Tolú Magangué Mompós
Coveñas Curumani
Lorica Sincelejo
4 Cereté El Banco **3**
Arboletes
Capurganá Montería
Acandí Necoclí Planeta
Golfo de Rica Caucasia
PANAMA *Uraba*
Turbo San Alberto Cúcuta
◆ *PNN* Chigorodó Pamplona
Pacific *Los Katios*
Ocean Travesía *PNN* Barrancabermeja Bucaramanga *PN*
Dabeiba *Paramillo* Girón *Tama*
Málaga Guicán
Jurado Santa Fé de Barichara
Antioquia San Gil El Cocuy
◆ *PNN Las* Puerto Socorro Tame
Orquídeas Berrio
Barbosa
Bahía Solano Medellín Rionegro Puerto Duitama
El Valle Bolívar Sta Bárbara Boyacá

N

100 km
100 miles

VENEZUELA

❼

❻

❺ Parque Nacional Natural Tayrona

Spend a few days chilling by the beach or trek the forests of Tayrona National Park. Busy in high season and at weekends, there are still lots of hidden coves and pristine scenery to explore. Plenty of wildlife can be found here as well, including monkeys and iguanas. Page 85.

❻ Ciudad Perdida

It takes several days to hike through the lush rainforest to the ruins of the lost city of the Tayrona and is an unforgettable experience. The final strenuous climb up 1200 slippery steps to the summit is not for the faint-hearted, but is well worthwhile. Page 88.

❼ La Guajira

Learn about Wayúu culture and traditions, visiting the very furthest reaches of Colombia in the remote desert peninsula of La Guajira. What it lacks in mod cons and creature comforts, it makes up for in wildlife and breathtaking landscapes. Page 103.

Barranquilla Carnival

Route planner

Cartagena is colonial Spain's finest legacy in the Americas, impressive in every respect. You could spend several days just exploring the city as there is so much to see. However, it is also a good base for visiting the Caribbean coast, with offshore islands, beaches, water sports and strange mud volcanoes nearby. Cartagena is the gateway to the Caribbean islands of San Andrés, a popular island resort, and to the charming neighbouring island of Providencia.

Northeast of Cartagena, the town of Barranquilla has its own attractions, including a spectacular carnival, perhaps the finest in Latin America after Rio de Janeiro. Continuing northeast is Santa Marta, currently undergoing a facelift to its colonial quarter and welcoming increasing numbers of tourists who explore the Tayrona National Park, the Sierra Nevada de Santa Marta and the beautiful beaches beyond. The remote Guajira Peninsula offers an adventurous trip to the communities and wildlife of the semi-desert at the extreme northeast of Colombia's Caribbean coast.

By contrast, the southwest corner, which adjoins Panama, is an adventure of a different kind: boats will take you to villages with tropical beaches, sheltering beneath the forests of Darién. Mompós is a superb colonial town that can be visited from Cartagena or other points in the region, but its relative isolation means that you will have to stay at least one night.

The other important inland city in the region is Valledupar, whose influence, in the form of *vallenato* music is heard on every street throughout the Caribbean. As well as the culture, Valledupar is worth a visit in its own right for the access it gives to the Sierra Nevada de Santa Marta.

One week

Start the week's explorations in historic **Cartagena** (see page 26), taking in the main sights and soaking up the atmosphere, then continue on to **Santa Marta** (see page 73), a convenient base for visiting the nearby national parks. Choose between chilling on the beach in pristine **Tayrona National Park** (see page 85) or trek through steaming jungles to reach Ciudad Perdida in **Sierra Nevada de Santa Marta** (see page 88).

Two weeks

From Tayrona/Sierra Nevada de Santa Marta continue on to **Riohacha** (see page 97), capital of the department of La Guajira, Colombia's rugged northeastern outpost. Make a quick stop at the flamingo sanctuary at **Camarones** (see page 98) on the way, then take a tour of the **Guajira Peninsula** (see page 103) visiting **Cabo de la Vela** (see page 104), **Macuira National Park** (see page 104) and **Punta Gallinas** (see page 105) .

Alternatively, after Cartagena, head west and spend a couple of days visiting **Arboletes** (see page 59) to wallow in the area's largest mud volcano and then take a boat from Tolú to visit the nearby **Islas de San Bernardo** (see page 59), part of a national park.

When
to go

… and when not to

Climate

Being so close to the equator, the climate varies little in Colombia and you will see plenty of sun all year round. Throughout most of the region there are no real seasons and temperature is dictated mainly by altitude. However, it often rains more from September to November and dirt tracks in remote areas such as the Guajira Peninsula can become impassable at this time. The best time for a visit is December to February, which are the driest months on average. The peak holiday seasons are: 15 December to mid- to late January; Easter; and 15 June to 31 August. During these periods prices rise significantly in the most popular places, and transport (including domestic flights), can be busy.

The islands of San Andrés and Providencia have a typical Caribbean climate that includes hurricane season from roughly June to November. The best weather on the islands is from December to April, but these months also attract the largest crowds.

Weather Caribbean Colombia (Cartagena)

January	February	March	April	May	June
29°C	29°C	30°C	30°C	30°C	30°C
23°C	24°C	25°C	25°C	26°C	26°C
4mm	3mm	2mm	22mm	90mm	100mm

July	August	September	October	November	December
30°C	30°C	30°C	30°C	30°C	30°C
26°C	26°C	25°C	25°C	25°C	24°C
80mm	110mm	130mm	220mm	130mm	30mm

Festivals

García Márquez once said, "five Colombians in a room invariably turns into a party". It could also be said that a couple of hundred Colombians in a village invariably turns into a fiesta. Colombians will use almost anything as a pretext for a celebration. Every city, town and village has at least three or four annual events in which local products and traditions are celebrated with music, dancing and raucous revelry (these are listed throughout the book). One of the most significant is the **Barranquilla Carnival** (see page 71) in February, which sees four days of street parties, spectacular parades, music and dancing. Easter is a local holiday time and almost every town has superb **Semana Santa** celebrations, Mompós (see page 56) chief among them. See also Festivals, page 125.

What to do

from diving coral reefs to exploring lost cities

The Colombian Caribbean region offers various activities, both inland and along its beautiful coastline. Outdoor pursuits, cultural activities and wildlife viewing, particularly birdwatching, are just some of the options available.

Birdwatching

Colombia, with nearly 1900 bird species, is great for birdwatching and several prime areas, such as **Ciénaga de Santa Marta** (page 82) and the flamingo sanctuary near **Riohacha** (page 97), are located in the Caribbean region. It's also good for wildlife viewing in general – the area is home to tortoises, monkeys and many species of iguana. **Colombia Birdwatch**, www.colombiabirdwatch.com, has tours and more information.

Diving and water sports

Many places along the coast, as well as the islands of **San Andrés** (page 109) and **Providencia** (page 115), are excellent for diving and other water sports. The aforementioned islands are home to the third largest barrier reef in the world, while **Taganga** (page 82), on the mainland, is a good place to get your diving certificate. **Poseidon Dive Center**, www.poseidondivecenter.com, in Taganga is a recommended operator.

Shopping tips

Colombia takes pride in its artisanal prowess, which can be seen in the handcrafted items on sale everywhere in the country, but with distinctive differences depending on the region. Ráquira in Boyacá Department is regarded as the centre of Colombian pottery, but the popular, brightly coloured folk art ceramics most associated with the country are made in Pitalito in the south and can be bought all over. Other good buys include hammocks in the north (especially around the Guajira Peninsula), leather goods in the south around Pasto, sisal-based textiles (known as *fique*), Panama hats, basketwork and gold (notably in Bogotá, Cartagena and Mompós). In most cases these items are very good value. A traditional *mochila* handbag, for example, which can cost hundreds of euros in Paris or Milan, can be bought for a song in Cartagena or Medellín. Bear this in mind when buying a handcrafted item in Colombia and do not haggle too much; your bargain may well be the only source of income for the vendor.

Horse riding

Away from the coast and in more remote locations such as the **Guajira Peninsula** (page 103), horse riding is popular and a great way of seeing the Colombian countryside. There are coffee fincas in the Caribbean region, many of which offer horse riding, as part of a visit to or stay on the coffee farm.

Trekking and walking

The varied terrain means that there is ample choice for the avid hiker, with everything from strenuous treks to gentle beach strolls to choose from. The epic six-day trek to **Ciudad Perdida** (page 88) in Sierra Nevada de Santa Marta is not to be missed, while **Tayrona National Park** (page 85), right on the Caribbean Sea, offers easier hikes with excellent sea views. In more remote locations, make sure you take local advice or hire a guide, and take plenty of water. **Karibana**, www. karibanacartagena.com, organizes walks in and around **Cartagena** (page 26).

Where to stay

from boutique hotels to hammocks

Colombia has a number of exceptional boutique hotels that are well worth seeking out. They are often in restored colonial buildings and not necessarily expensive. Budget accommodation is improving and an increasing number of backpacker hostels are opening up. There is a small network of youth hostels, of varying quality, which is used extensively by Colombian groups and welcomes international members (see below).

The Colombian hotel federation, **COTELCO** ⓘ *www.cotelco.org*, has a list of authorized prices for member hotels, which can be consulted at tourist offices. In theory, all hotels should be registered, but this is not always the case, particularly with cheaper hotels. Most hotels in Colombia charge for extra beds for children, up to a maximum (usually) of four beds per room. Prices are normally displayed at reception, but in quiet periods it is always worth negotiating. Ask to see the room before committing.

When booking a hotel from an airport or bus station, try to speak to the hotel yourself; most will understand at least simple English and possibly French, German or Italian. If you use an official tourist agent you will probably pay a little more as a booking fee. If you accept help from anyone else, you could be putting yourself at risk.

'Motels' are almost always pay-by-the-hour 'love hotels' for use by illicit lovers, couples still living with their parents, or prostitutes and their clients. Most of the time, especially with the more expensive drive-in ones on the

Price codes

Where to stay	Restaurants
$$$$ over US$150	$$$ over US$12
$$$ US$66-150	$$ US$7-12
$$ US$30-65	$ US$6 and under
$ under US$30	Price for a two-course meal for one person, excluding drinks or service charge.
Price for a double room in high season, including taxes.	

outskirts of town, the names will provide an obvious enough clue (eg 'Passion Motel'), but this is not always the case.

In cheaper hotels, beware of electric shower heaters, which can be dangerous due to faulty wiring.

Toilets may suffer from inadequate water supplies. In all cases, however, do not flush paper down the toilet bowl but use the bin provided. Carry toilet paper with you as cheaper establishments as well as restaurants, bars, etc, may not provide it, or make an additional charge for it.

Camping

Local tourist authorities have lists of official campsites, but they are seldom signposted on main roads, so can be hard to find. Permission to camp with a tent, campervan or car may be granted by landowners in less populated areas. Many *haciendas* have armed guards protecting their property, which can add to your safety. Do not camp on private land without permission. Those in campervans can camp by the roadside, but it is not particularly safe and it can be difficult to find a secluded spot. If you have a vehicle, it is possible to camp at truck drivers' restaurants or sometimes at police or army posts. Check very carefully before deciding to camp: you may be exposing yourself to significant danger. Some hostels, particularly in rural areas, also offer camping and often provide tents and other equipment at an additional cost, but are still cheaper than dorm beds.

Homestays

In many places, it is possible to stay with a local family; check with the local tourist office to see what is available. This is a good option for those interested in learning Spanish informally in a family environment. However, if you take formal classes, you should have a student visa (see Visas and immigration, page 132).

Youth hostels

La Federación Colombiana de Albergues Juveniles (FCAJ) ① *Cra 7, No 6-10, Bogotá, T280 3041, hostelling@fcaj.org.co*, is affiliated to **Hostelling International** ① *www.hihostels.com*. **Colombian Hostels** ① *www.colombianhostels.com.co*, has a good network of 41 members around the country. **Hostel Trail Latin America** ① *Cra 11, No 4-16, Popayán, T831 7871, www.hosteltrail.com*, is an online network of hostels and tour companies in South America providing information on locally run businesses for backpackers and independent travellers.

Food
& drink

from lobster soup to fried plantain and coconut rice

Colombia has yet to reach international renown for its cuisine, but food is becoming more of a draw. Even though you can now find most regional specialities in all the major cities, there are many local variations to sample throughout the country.

A standard item on the menu is *sancocho*, a meat stock (may be fish on the coast) with potato, corn (on the cob), yucca, sweet potato and plantain. *Arroz con pollo* (chicken and rice), popular across Latin American, is excellent in Colombia. *Carne asada* (grilled beefsteak), usually an inexpensive cut, is served with *papas fritas* (chips) or rice and you can ask for a vegetable of the day. *Sobrebarriga* (belly of beef) is served with varieties of potato in a tomato and onion sauce. *Huevos pericos* (eggs scrambled with onions and tomatoes) are a popular, cheap and nourishing snack available almost anywhere, especially favoured for breakfast. *Tamales* are meat pies made by folding a maize dough round chopped pork mixed with potato, rice, peas, onions and eggs wrapped in banana leaves (which you don't eat) and steamed. Other ingredients may be added such as olives, garlic, cloves and paprika. Colombians eat *tamales* for breakfast with hot chocolate. *Empanadas* are another popular snack; these are made with chicken or various other meats, or vegetarian filling, inside a maize dough and deep fried in oil. *Patacones* are cakes of mashed and baked *platano* (large green banana). *Arepas* are standard throughout Colombia; these are flat maize griddle cakes often served instead of bread or as an alternative. *Pan de bono* is cheese flavoured bread. *Almojábanas*, a kind of sour milk/cheese bread roll, are great for breakfast when freshly made. *Buñuelos* are 4- to 6-cm balls of wheat flour and eggs mixed and deep-fried, best when still warm. *Arequipe* is a sugar-based brown syrup used with desserts and in confectionary, universally savoured by Colombians. *Brevas* (figs) with *arequipe* are one of the most popular desserts.

Regional specialities

Fish is naturally a speciality in the coastal regions. In *arroz con coco* the rice is prepared with coconut. *Cazuela de mariscos*, a soup/stew of shellfish and white fish, maybe including octopus and squid, is especially good. *Sancocho de pescado* is a fish stew with vegetables, usually simpler and cheaper than *cazuela*. *Chipichipi*, a small clam found along the coast in Barranquilla and Santa Marta, is a standard local dish served with rice. *Empanada* (or *arepa*) *de huevo*, is deep fried with eggs in the middle and is a good light meal. *Canasta de coco* is a good local sweet: pastry containing coconut custard flavoured with wine and topped by meringue.

Restaurants

In Cartagena you will find a limitless choice of menu and price. Other large towns have a good range of specialist restaurants and all the usual fast-food outlets, both Colombian and international. In the smaller towns and villages not catering for tourists, you'll find a modest selection of places to eat. Be sure to check opening times for the evenings, particularly at weekends; some places may close around 1800. On Sundays it can be particularly difficult to eat in a restaurant and even hotel restaurants may be closed.

Most of the bigger cities have specific vegetarian restaurants and you will find them listed in the travelling text. They are normally open only for lunch. In towns and villages you will have to ask for special food to be prepared.

The main Colombian meal of the day is at lunchtime, the *almuerzo* or *menú ejecutivo/del día*, with soup, main course and fruit juice or *gaseosa* (soft drink). If you are economizing, ask for the *plato del día*, *bandeja* or *plato corriente* (just the main dish). This can be found everywhere and restaurants usually display the menu and cost in the window or on a board.

The cheapest food can be found in markets (when they are open), from street stalls in downtown areas and at transport terminals, but bear in mind it might not be safe or agree with you. The general rules apply: keep away from uncooked food and salads, and eat fruit you have peeled yourself. Watch what the locals are eating as a guide to the best choice. Having said that, take it easy with dishes that are unfamiliar especially if you have arrived from a different climate or altitude. Wash it down with something out of a sealed bottle. If you find the fresh fruit drinks irresistible, you will have to take your chances! See Health, page 126.

Drinks

Colombian coffee is always mild. *Tinto*, the national small cup of black coffee, is taken at all hours. The name is misleading; don't expect to get a glass of red wine. If you want it strong, ask for *café cargado*; a *tinto doble* is a large cup of black coffee. Coffee with milk is called *café perico*; *café con leche* is a mug of milk with coffee added. If you want a coffee with less milk, order *tinto y leche aparte* and they will bring the milk separately.

Tea is popular but herbal rather than Indian or Chinese: ask for *(bebida) aromática*; flavours include *limonaria*, *orquídea* and *manzanilla*. If you want Indian tea, *té Lipton en agua* should do the trick. *Té de menta* (mint tea) is another of many varieties available but you may have to go to an upmarket café or *casa de té*, which can be found in all of the bigger cities. Chocolate is also drunk: *chocolate Santafereño* is often taken during the afternoon with snacks and cheese. *Agua de panela* (hot water with unrefined sugar) is a common beverage, also made with limes, milk or cheese.

Bottled soft drinks are universal and standard, commonly called *gaseosas*. If you want non-carbonated, ask for *sin gas*. Again you will find that many fruits are used for bottled drinks. Water comes in bottles, cartons and small plastic packets, or even plastic bags: all safer than out of the tap, although tap water is generally of a reasonable quality.

Many acceptable brands of beer are produced, until recently almost all produced by the Bavaria group. Each region has a preference for different brands. The most popular are **Aguila**, **Club Colombia**, **Costeña** and **Poker**.

A traditional drink in Colombia is *chicha*. It is corn-based but sugar and/or *panela* are added and it is boiled. It is served as a non-alcoholic beverage, but if allowed to ferment over several days, and especially if kept in the fridge for a while, it becomes very potent.

The local rum is good and cheap; ask for *ron*, not *aguardiente*. One of the best rums is **Ron Viejo de Caldas**, another (dark) is **Ron Medellín**. Try *canelazo*, cold or hot rum with water, sugar, lime and cinnamon. As common as rum is *aguardiente* (literally 'fire water'), a white spirit distilled from sugar cane. There are two types, with *anís* (aniseed) or without. Local table wines include **Isabella**; none is very good. Wine is very expensive: as much as US$15 in restaurants for an acceptable bottle of Chilean or Argentine wine, more for European and other wines.

Fruit and juices

Colombia has an exceptional range and quality of fruit – another aspect of the diversity of altitude and climate. Fruits familiar in northern and Mediterranean climates, though with some differences, include: *manzanas* (apples); *bananos* (bananas); *uvas* (grapes); *limones* (limes; lemons, the larger yellow variety, are rarely seen); *mangos* (mangoes); *melones* (melons); *naranjas* (oranges; usually green or yellow in Colombia); *duraznos* (peaches); and *peras* (pears).

Then there are the local fruits: *chirimoyas* (a green fruit, white inside with pips); *curuba* (banana passion fruit); *feijoa* (a green fruit with white flesh, high in vitamin C); *guayaba* (guava); *guanábana* (soursop); *lulo* (a small orange fruit); *maracuyá* (passion fruit); *mora* (literally 'black berry' but dark red more like a loganberry); *papaya*; the delicious *pitahaya* (taken either as an appetizer or dessert); *sandía* (watermelon); *tomate de árbol* (tree tomato, several varieties normally used as a fruit); and many more.

All of these fruits can be served as juices, either with milk (hopefully fresh) or water (hopefully bottled or sterilized). Most hotels and restaurants are careful about this and you can watch the drinks being prepared on street stalls. Fruit yoghurts are nourishing and cheap; **Alpina** brand is good; *crema* style is best. Also, **Kumis** is a type of liquid yoghurt. Another drink you must try is *champús*, a corn base with fruit, *panela*, cloves and cinnamon added.

Menu reader

Regional specialities are described on page 18. Some of the standard items on the menu are:

Ajiaco	A thick soup made with potatoes, chicken and cream.
Almojábanas	Sour milk/cheese bread roll, great for breakfast when freshly made.
Arepas	Flat maize griddle cakes found throughout the country and often served as an alternative to bread.
Arequipe	Sugar-based brown syrup used for desserts and confectionary, universally loved by Colombians.
Arroz con pollo	Chicken and rice, one of the standard Latin American dishes, is excellent in Colombia.
Brevas	Figs – served with *arequipe* as a popular dessert.
Buñuelos	4-6 cm balls of wheat flour and egg dough, deep-fried and best when still warm.
Carne asada	Grilled beefsteak, usually an inexpensive cut, served with *papas fritas* (chips) or rice and a vegetable of the day.
Chicha	Corn-based drink with sugar and/or *panela* added.
Champús	Corn-based drink with fruit, *panela*, cloves and cinnamon.
Empanadas	Maize pasties, filled with chicken, meat or vegetables and deep fried in oil. A popular snack.
Huevos pericos	Eggs scrambled with onions and tomatoes. A popular, cheap and nourishing snack available almost everywhere, especially for breakfast.
Pan de bono	Cheese-flavoured bread.
Patacones	Cakes of mashed and baked *platano* (large green banana).
Sancocho	A meat stock (may be fish on the coast) with potato, corn (on the cob), yucca, sweet potato and plantain.
Sobrebarriga	Belly of beef served with varieties of potato in a tomato and onion sauce.
Tamales	Meat pies made from chopped pork, potato, rice, peas, onions and eggs in a maize dough. They are wrapped in banana leaves (which you don't eat) and steamed. Other ingredients may include olives, garlic, cloves and paprika. In certain areas Colombians eat *tamales* for breakfast with hot chocolate.

ON THE ROAD

Improve your travel photography

Taking pictures is a highlight for many travellers, yet too often the results turn out to be disappointing. Steve Davey, author of Footprint's *Travel Photography*, sets out his top rules for coming home with pictures you can be proud of.

Before you go
Don't waste precious travelling time and do your research before you leave. Find out what festivals or events might be happening or which day the weekly market takes place, and search online image sites such as Flickr to see whether places are best shot at the beginning or end of the day, and what vantage points you should consider.

Get up early
The quality of the light will be better in the few hours after sunrise and again before sunset – especially in the tropics when the sun will be harsh and unforgiving in the middle of the day. Sometimes seeing the sunrise is a part of the whole travel experience: sleep in and you will miss more than just photographs.

Stop and think
Don't just click away without any thought. Pause for a few seconds before raising the camera and ask yourself what you are trying to show with your photograph. Think about what things you need to include in the frame to convey this meaning. Be prepared to move around your subject to get the best angle. Knowing the point of your picture is the first step to making sure that the person looking at the picture will know it too.

Compose your picture
Avoid simply dumping your subject in the centre of the frame every time you take a picture. If you compose with it to one side, then your picture can look more balanced. This will also allow you to show a significant background and make the picture more meaningful. A good rule of thumb is to place your subject or any significant detail a third of the way into the frame; facing into the frame not out of it.

This rule also works for landscapes. Compose with the horizon two-thirds of the way up the frame if the foreground is the most interesting part of the picture; one-third of the way up if the sky is more striking.

Don't get hung up with this so-called Rule of Thirds, though. Exaggerate it by pushing your subject out to the edge of the frame if it makes a more interesting picture; or if the sky is dull in a landscape, try cropping with the horizon near the very top of the frame.

Fill the frame
If you are going to focus on a detail or even a person's face in a close-up portrait, then be bold and make sure that you fill the frame. This is often a case of physically getting in close. You can use a telephoto setting on a zoom lens but this can lead to pictures looking quite flat; moving in close is a lot more fun!

Interact with people

If you want to shoot evocative portraits then it is vital to approach people and seek permission in some way, even if it is just by smiling at someone. Spend a little time with them and they are likely to relax and look less stiff and formal. Action portraits where people are doing something, or environmental portraits, where they are set against a significant background, are a good way to achieve relaxed portraits. Interacting is a good way to find out more about people and their lives, creating memories as well as photographs.

Focus carefully

Your camera can focus quicker than you, but it doesn't know which part of the picture you want to be in focus. If your camera is using the centre focus sensor then move the camera so it is over the subject and half press the button, then, holding it down, recompose the picture. This will lock the focus. Take the now correctly focused picture when you are ready.

Another technique for accurate focusing is to move the active sensor over your subject. Some cameras with touch-sensitive screens allow you to do this by simply clicking on the subject.

Leave light in the sky

Most good night photography is actually taken at dusk when there is some light and colour left in the sky; any lit portions of the picture will balance with the sky and any ambient lighting. There is only a very small window when this will happen, so get into position early, be prepared and keep shooting and reviewing the results. You can take pictures after this time, but avoid shots of tall towers in an inky black sky; crop in close on lit areas to fill the frame.

Bring it home safely

Digital images are inherently ephemeral: they can be deleted or corrupted in a heartbeat. The good news though is they can be copied just as easily. Wherever you travel, you should have a backup strategy. Cloud backups are popular, but make sure that you will have access to fast enough Wi-Fi. If you use RAW format, then you will need some sort of physical back-up. If you don't travel with a laptop or tablet, then you can buy a backup drive that will copy directly from memory cards.

Recently updated and available in both digital and print formats, Footprint's Travel Photography by Steve Davey covers everything you need to know about travelling with a camera, including simple post-processing. More information is available at www.footprinttravelguides.com

Cartagena
& around

Cartagena

Besides being Colombia's top tourist destination and a World Heritage Site, Cartagena is one of the hottest, most vibrant and beautiful cities in South America. It combines superb weather and a sparkling stretch of coastline with an eclectic mix of Caribbean, African and Spanish tastes and sounds. Nuggets of history can be found around every corner and in every palm-shaded courtyard of this most romantic of places. With exquisitely preserved architecture, excellent museums and fine dining, it's a city to be savoured.

The walled city is a labyrinth of colourful squares, churches, mansions and pastel-coloured houses along narrow cobbled streets. The San Diego quarter and Plaza Santo Domingo perhaps best capture the lure of Cartagena; don't miss a drink at night in the cafés here.

Cartagena is also a popular beach resort with modern high-rise hotels lining the seafront at Bocagrande and the road to Barranquilla. Just offshore in the bay, sandy islands are lapped by the turquoise sea.

Essential Cartagena

Finding your feet

The colonial heart of Cartagena, El Centro, lies within 12 km of ramparts at the northern end of the Bahía de Cartagena. Most of the upmarket hotels and restaurants are found here. Less touristy is the Getsemaní neighbourhood, where the colonial buildings house many budget hotels. Immediately adjoining Getsemaní is the downtown sector known as La Matuna. Beyond this central area the city sprawls for 10 km to the north, south and east. In the bay are several low, sandy islands, while further south, the Islas del Rosario are glistening examples of what tropical islands should look like.

Getting around

Within the city green and white Metrocar buses are a recommended way to get to all areas, US$1; taxis are also quite cheap and may be more convenient. The walled city should, however, be explored on foot; take your time and don't fret about getting lost in the narrow streets. A stroll along the ramparts will give you an excellent overview. Boats from the Muelle Turístico go to outlying beaches and islands.

Safety

Carry your passport, or a photocopy, at all times. Failure to present it on police request can result in imprisonment and fines. Generally, the central areas are safe and friendly (although Getsemaní is less secure), but should you require the police, there is a station in Barrio Manga. Beware of drug pushers on the beaches, pickpockets in crowded areas and bag/camera snatchers on quiet Sunday mornings. At the bus station, do not be pressurized into a hotel recommendation different from your own choice.

When to go

The weather is warm year-round; the hottest and wettest months are between August and November. Cartagena can become very crowded around Christmas and Easter and during its numerous festivals.

Time required

Allow a couple of days to explore the city and a few more to relax on the beaches.

The streets within the historic centre are narrow. Each block has a different name, which can cause confusion, but don't worry: the thing to do is to wander aimlessly, savouring the street scenes and allow the great sights to take you by surprise. Most of the 'great houses' can be visited and some churches are open to the public for most of the day; others only at 1800.

The ramparts
www.patrimoniodecartagena.com/es.

In addition to being a spectacular feature of Cartagena, the city walls make a great walk and are an excellent way to visit many of the attractions inside the old city. A good place to start is the **Baluarte San Francisco Javier** from where, with a few ups and downs, the circuit is continuous to **La India Catalina**. From this point, there are two further sections along the lagoons to the **Puente Román**. The final section of the circuit along the Calle del Arsenal can be completed through the **Playa de Barahona**, a bayside park, which is busy at weekends. The entire walk takes about 1½ hours, although if you bring a camera it can take considerably longer. It is a spectacular walk in the morning around 0600 and equally at sunset. At many points you can drop down to see the sights detailed in the tour of the old city below.

Outer city
The **Puente Román** is the bridge that leads from Manga Island (with its shipping terminals) into the area of Getsemaní, characterized by its *casas bajas* (low houses) in which the artisan classes lived. Today, many of these one-storey houses are being restored and there is a concentration of hotels and restaurants here. The chapel of **San Roque**, early 17th century, is at the eastern end of Calle Media Luna, near the hospital of Espíritu Santo. Just across the **Playa Pedregal** from here is the Laguna de San Lázaro and the **Puente Heredia**, which leads to the Castillo San Felipe de Barajas (see below). North of Calle Media Luna is the modern downtown sector, known as **La Matuna**, where vendors crowd the pavements and alleys between modern commercial buildings. Several middle-range hotels are in this district, between Avenidas Venezuela and Lemaitre.

In an interesting plaza, is the church of **Santísima Trinidad**, built 1643 but not consecrated until 1839. Near the church, at No 10 Calle Guerrero, lived Pedro Romero, who set the revolution of 1811 going by coming out into the street shouting 'Long Live Liberty'. His statue can be seen outside La Trinidad. Along Calle Larga is the monastery of **San Francisco**. The church was built in 1590 after the pirate Martin Côte had destroyed an earlier church built in 1559. The first Inquisitors lodged at the monastery. From its courtyard a crowd surged into the streets claiming Independence from Spain

> **Tip...**
> Weekends and holidays are the best times for photography as traffic is minimal.

on 11 November 1811. The main part of the monastery has now been turned into business premises – take a look at the cloister garden as you pass by. Good-value fixed-price handicrafts are sold in the grounds of the monastery and, at the back, is the Centro Comercial Getsemaní, a busy shopping centre.

On the corner of Calle Larga, formerly part of the Franciscan complex, is the **Iglesia de la Tercera Orden**, a busy church with a fine wooden roof of unusual design and some brightly painted niche figures. The church and monastery front on to the Avenida del Mercado on the other side of which is the **Centro Internacional de Convenciones**. It holds gatherings of up to 4000 people and is frequently used for local and international conventions. It was built in 1972 on the site of the old colourful market, now banished to the interior part of the city. Although the severe fort-like structure is more or less in keeping with the surrounding historic walls and bastions, not everyone believes this is an improvement. When not in use, ask for a guide to show you around.

Immediately to the north is **Plaza de la Independencia**, with the landscaped **Parque del Centenario** next to it. The **Paseo de los Mártires** runs alongside the plaza, by the water, flanked by the busts of nine patriots executed in the square on 24 February 1816 by the royalist Pablo Morillo after he had retaken the city. At the western end of the paseo is a tall clock tower, **Torre del Reloj**, often used as the symbol of Cartagena. To the left is the **Muelle de los Pegasos** (Muelle Turístico) from where the tourist boats leave. Under the clock tower is the **Puerta del Reloj**: these three arches are the principal entrance to the inner walled city.

Inner city

Inside the Puerta del Reloj is the **Plaza de los Coches**. As in almost all the plazas of Cartagena, its arcades offer refuge from the tropical sun. At one time this plaza was the slave market, and later it was the departure point for carriages (*coches*), which could be hired for local journeys. On the west side of this plaza is the **Portal de los Dulces**, a favourite meeting place where you can still buy all manner of local sweets and delicacies. It also has a number of good bars, often quite buzzing even during the day.

Plaza de la Aduana has a statue of Columbus in the centre and the **Casa de la Aduana** along the wall, originally the tax office and now part of the city administration as the **Palacio Municipal**. Opposite is the **Casa del Marqués del Premio Real**, which was the residence of the representative of the Spanish king. In the corner of the wall is the **Museo de Arte Moderno** ⓘ *www.mamcartagena.org, Mon-Fri 0900-1200, 1500-1900, Sat 1000-1300, US$1.75, free Wed*, a collection of the work of modern Colombian artists. There is a museum shop.

Past the museum is the **Convento de San Pedro Claver** ⓘ *daily 0900-1700, US$4.50*, and the church and monastery of the same name, built by Jesuits in 1603 and later dedicated to San Pedro Claver, a monk in the monastery, who died in 1654 and was canonized 235 years later. He was called *El Esclavo de los Esclavos*, or *El Apóstol de los Negros*, and used to beg from door to door for money to give to the black slaves brought to the city. His body is in an illuminated glass coffin set in the high marble altar, and his cell and the balcony from which he kept watch for

Cartagena historic centre

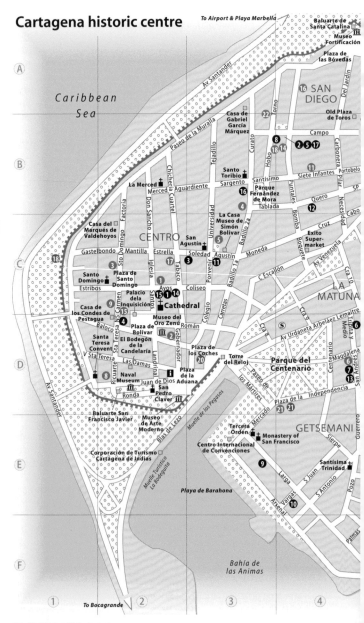

To Airport & Playa Marbella

Baluarte de Santa Catalina
Museo Fortificación
Plaza de las Bóvedas

SAN DIEGO

Old Plaza de Toros

Caribbean Sea

Av Santander

Paseo de la Muralla

Casa de Gabriel García Márquez

Campo

La Merced

Chichería Cuartel

Merced Aguardiente

Don Sancho

Factoría

Santo Toribio

Sargento

Parque Fernández de Mora

Casa del Marqués de Valdehoyos

Gastelbondo

Sto Domingo

Mantilla

Iglesia

Estrella

Universidad

San Agustín

Soledad

La Casa Museo de Simón Bolívar

Éxito Supermarket

CENTRO

Porvenir

Moneda

Santo Domingo

Plaza de Santo Domingo

Estribos

Casa de los Condes de Pestagua

Palacio de la Inquisición

Cathedral

Coliseo

Badillo la

C Escallón

Carretas

LA MATUNA

Museo del Oro Zenú

Román

El Bodegón de la Candelaría

Plaza de Bolívar

Gobernador

Plaza de los Coches

Parque del Centenario

Santa Teresa Convent

Sta Teresa

Baloco

Las Damas

Naval Museum

Ronda

San Pedro Claver

Juan de Dios

Plaza de la Aduana

Torre del Reloj

Plaza de la Independencia

Baluarte San Francisco Javier

Museo de Arte Moderno

Blas de Lezo

Muelle de los Pegasos

Tercera Orden

Monastery of San Francisco

GETSEMANI

Corporación de Turismo Cartagena de Indias

Centro Internacional de Convenciones

Santísima Trinidad

Larga

Muelle Turístico La Bodeguita

Playa de Barahona

Arsenal

Vargas

Bahía de las Animas

To Bocagrande

slave ships are shown to visitors. There are brightly coloured birds in the small monastery garden. Several upstairs rooms form a museum, with many interesting items linked or unrelated to Pedro Claver. In the pottery room, for example, is the chair used by the Pope on his visit to Cartagena in 1986. In another room there are several old maps, one of which shows the Caribbean maritime boundaries of Colombia, topical in that disputes with Nicaragua over San Andrés still persist today, despite an international court ruling in favour of Colombia.

Even if you're not walking the ramparts (see above), it is well worthwhile climbing up the **Baluarte San Francisco Javier** for a good view of the city and the Caribbean. There is a **Museo Naval del Caribe** ⓘ *C San Juan de Dios No3-62, T5-664 2440, www. museonavaldelcaribe.com, daily 1000-1730, US$2.75, discount for children*, with maps, models and displays of armaments, near the Baluarte.

On the corner of Calle Ricaurte is the convent of **Santa Teresa**, founded in 1609 by a rich benefactor as a convent for Carmelite nuns. It had various uses subsequently, as a prison, a military barracks, a school and in the 1970s, was occupied by the police. It was purchased by the Banco Central as a heritage investment and has been converted into a hotel, the **Charleston Santa Teresa** ⓘ *Cra 3, No 31-23, www.hotelcharlestonsantateresa.com.* It is possible to visit the public areas of the hotel and admire the tasteful work of restoration. There is a great view from the roof.

El Bodegón de la Candelaria ⓘ *C Las Damas No 3-64*, was an elegant colonial residence. It has been faithfully

BACKGROUND
Fortifying Cartagena

The full name of Cartagena is Cartagena de Indias, a reminder that the early Spanish navigators believed they had reached the Far East. The city was founded by Pedro de Heredia on 13 January 1533 and was built by the Spaniards on an island separated from the mainland by marshes and lagoons, close to a prominent hill. It was near to the mouth of the Río Magdalena, the route to the interior of the continent, and thus became one of the most important depots for merchandise arriving from Spain and for treasure collected from the Americas to be sent back. The Bahía de Cartagena, which is 15 km long and 5 km wide, was protected by several low, sandy islands, which formed natural sea defences. There were originally just two approaches to the bay – Bocagrande, at the northern end of Tierrabomba island, and Bocachica, a narrow channel to the south – thus making it a perfect place for a harbour and, more importantly at the time, easy to defend against attack. The city's wealth made it a prize target for French and English privateers operating in the Caribbean, including Sir Francis Drake who took the city in 1586. In response, a series of forts were built to protect Cartagena from raids from the sea, and formidable walls were constructed around the city, making it almost impregnable.

The harbour was protected by fortifications on Tierrabomba, Barú, Bocagrande and on the mainland, while the Puente Román, which connected the old city with Manga island to the southeast, was defended by three forts:

restored and has some fine panelling and period furniture. A small shrine in one of the rooms marks the place where the Virgin appeared to a priest who was living there at the time.

One block away is **Plaza de Bolívar** with an equestrian statue of the Liberator in the centre and attractive gardens. Formerly it was the Plaza de la Inquisición, with the **Palacio de la Inquisición** ① *www.muhca.gov.co, Mon-Sat 0900-1800, Sun 1000-1600, US$6*, on its west side. First established in 1610, the jurisdiction of this tribunal extended to Venezuela and Panama, and at least 800 were sentenced to death here. The present building dates from 1706 and has a small window overlooking the plaza where the public were informed of the sentences. The stone entrance with its coats of arms and ornate wooden door is well preserved, and the whole building, with its balconies, cloisters and patios, is a fine example of colonial baroque. The small museum contains photos of Cartagena from the 20th century, paintings of historical figures and a torture chamber (with reproductions of actual instruments). Of special interest are the model of Cartagena in 1808, copies of Alexander Von Humboldt's maps showing the link he discovered between the Orinoco and Amazon rivers (*Canal de Casiquiare*) and of the Maypures rapids on the Orinoco – note that the longitude lines on the maps are west of Paris not Greenwich.

San Sebastián del Pastelillo, built between 1558 and 1567 (now occupied by the Club de Pesca), San Lorenzo and the very powerful Castillo San Felipe de Barajas inland to the east. Yet another fort, La Tenaza, protected the northern point of the walled city from a direct attack from the open sea. In 1650, the Spaniards built the 145-km-long Canal del Dique connecting the city to the Río Magdalena and allowing free access for ships from the upriver ports. The city suffered a devastating raid by the French, led by Baron de Pointis and Jean Baptiste Ducasse, in 1697, but returned to prosperity during the 18th century as one of the most important cities in the newly formed Viceroyalty of New Granada. Following an unsuccessful but sustained attack by Admiral Edward Vernon in 1741, Bocagrande was blocked by an underwater wall, thus leaving only one entrance to the harbour.

The huge walls that encircle the old city were started early in the 17th century and finished by 1735. They were on average 12 m high and 17 m thick, with six gates. Besides barracks, they contained a water reservoir. The old city was in two sections, outer and inner, divided by a wall. The artisan classes lived in one-storey houses in the outer city, in an area known as Getsemaní, where many colonial buildings survive. The inner city, or El Centro, was originally occupied by the high officials and nobility, with the clerks, merchants, priests and military living in San Diego at the northern end.

Cartagena declared its Independence from Spain in 1811. A year later Bolívar used the city as a jumping-off point for his Magdalena campaign. After heroic resistance, Cartagena was retaken by the royalists under General Pablo Morillo in 1815. It was finally freed by the patriots in 1821.

On the opposite side of the Plaza de Bolívar is the Museo del Oro Zenú ⓘ www.banrepcultural.org/gold-museum/regional-museums, Tue-Fri 1000-1300, 1500-1900, Sat 1000-1300, 1400-1700 Sun 1100-1600, free, which focuses on the gold and pottery of the Zenú area to the south of Cartagena in the marshlands of the Sinú, San Jorge and Magdalena rivers. This area was densely populated between the second and 10th centuries during which time the gold working skills of the people were developed to a high level. Early drainage systems are featured, as is the advanced level of weaving techniques using the cañafleche and other fresh water reeds. Goldworking can still be seen today at Mompós at the northern edge of the Zenú region (see page 55).

The cathedral, in the northeast corner of Plaza de Bolívar, begun in 1575, was partially destroyed by Francis Drake. Reconstruction was finished by 1612, but significant alterations were made between 1912 and 1923. It has a severe exterior, with a fine doorway, and a simply decorated interior. See the gilded 18th-century altar, the Carrara marble pulpit and the elegant arcades which sustain the central nave.

Across the street is the Palacio de la Proclamación named after the declaration of Independence of the State of Cartagena in November 1811. Before that it was the local governor's residence, and was also where Simón Bolívar stayed in 1826.

The building was restored in 1950. The adjacent plaza has interesting local art and sculpture on display daily in high season.

The church and monastery of **Santo Domingo**, built 1570 to 1579 is now a seminary. The old monastery was replaced by the present one in the 17th century. Inside, a miracle-making image of Christ, carved towards the end of the 16th century, is set on a baroque 19th-century altar. This is a very interesting neighbourhood, where very little has changed since the 16th century. In Calle Santo Domingo, No 33-29, is one of the great patrician houses of Cartagena, the **Casa de los Condes de Pestagua**, which was once the Colegio del Sagrado Corazón de Jesús and is now a boutique hotel (**Casa de Pestagua**, see page 39). It has a fine colonnaded courtyard, marble floors and magnificent palm trees in the centre garden. Beside the church is the **Plaza de Santo Domingo**, one of the most popular corners of Cartagena, with restaurants, bars and cafés. A sculpture by Fernando Botero, *Gertrudis*, or *La Gorda*, is in the plaza and creates an interesting juxtaposition between the colonial and the modern.

North of Santo Domingo at Calle de la Factoría 36-57 is the magnificent **Casa del Marqués de Valdehoyos**, originally owned by the Marqués, who had the lucrative licences to import slaves and flour. The woodcarving is some of the best in Cartagena: the ceilings, chandeliers, wooden arches and balustrading are unique. The views of the city from the fine upper floor balconies are also recommended. It is used for cultural events and conferences.

A short walk northeast is the plaza, church and convent of **La Merced**, founded 1618. The convent was a prison during Morillo's reign of terror. Its church is now the **Teatro Heredia**, which has been beautifully restored.

Two blocks east is Calle de la Universidad, at the end of which is the monastery of **San Agustín**, built in 1580, currently the Universidad de Cartagena. From its chapel, the pirate Baron de Pointis stole a 500-pound silver sepulchre. It was returned by the King of France, but the citizens melted it down to pay their troops during the siege by Morillo in 1815. There is a luxury hotel here, **Casa San Agustín** ⓘ *C de la Universidad No 36-44, www.hotelcasasanagustin.com.*

One block along Calle de San Agustín is **La Casa Museo de Simón Bolívar**, which houses a collection of memorabilia in the first Cartagena house he stayed in; it's now part of the **Biblioteca Bartolomé Calvo** owned by the Banco de la República.

One block along Badillo (Carrera 7) is the church of **Santo Toribio de Mogrovejo** ⓘ *Mass Mon-Fri 0630, 1200, 1815, Sat 0630, 1200, 1800 and Sun 0800, 1000, 1800, 1900, closed at other times.* Building began in 1729. In 1741, during Admiral Vernon's siege, a cannon ball fell into the church during Mass and lodged in one of the central columns; the ball is now in a recess in the west wall. The font of Carrara marble in the Sacristy is a masterpiece. There is a beautiful carved ceiling in *mudéjar* style above the main altar with a rear-lighted figure of Christ.

The church and monastery of **Santa Clara de Assisi** is close by. It was built 1617-1621 and has been spectacularly restored. It is now the **Santa Clara Hotel** ⓘ *C del Torno, No 39-29, www.sofitel.com*, but this is one you must see. Behind the hotel is the orange **Casa de Gabriel García Márquez**, the former Cartagena home of Colombia's most famous author, on the corner of Calle del Curato.

Beyond the Santa Clara is the **Plaza de Las Bóvedas**, whose walls, built in 1799, are 12 m high and 15-18 m thick. At the base of the wall are 23 dungeons, now containing tourist shops. An illuminated underground passage and a drawbridge lead from Las Bóvedas to the fortress of **La Tenaza**, which guarded the approach to the city from the coast to the northeast. Next to La Tenaza is the Baluarte de Santa Catalina, which houses the **Museo Fortificación de Santa Catalina** ⓘ *www. patrimoniodecartagena.com, daily 0800-1800, US$2.50, children US$1.35*, inside the walls themselves. Towards the sea is a bank (*espiga*) leading to a jetty used in colonial times when the water came up to the walls, as shown on the 1808 map displayed in the **Palacio de la Inquisición**. All the land below the walls has since been reclaimed, with sports fields, recreational areas and the Avenida Santander/Paseo de la Muralla, a busy bypass to the city.

Casa de Núñez ⓘ *Tue-Fri 0900-1700, Sat-Sun 1000-1600, free*, just outside the walls of La Tenaza in El Cabrero district, was the home of Rafael Núñez, four-time president of Colombia. He wrote the national anthem and established the constitution of 1886, to which there is a monument in the small park beside the lagoon. Núñez' grandiose marble tomb is in the delightful small **Ermita El Cabrero** church opposite.

Closer to the centre, where a major road leads into the city, is a roundabout, in the centre of which is the monument to **La India Catalina**, Pedro de Heredia's indigenous interpreter in the early days of the Spanish conquest. A miniature of this statue is given to the winner of the annual Cartagena film festival – a Colombian 'Oscar'.

East of the historic centre

a formidable fortress, a ruined convent and great views

Castillo San Felipe de Barajas
San Lázaro hill across the Puente Heredia from the old city, daily 0800-1730, US$8, guides available.

Located 41 m above sea level on San Felipe de Barajas is the largest Spanish fort built in the Americas. Under the huge structure is a network of tunnels cut into the rock, lined with living rooms and offices. Visitors pass through these and on to the top of the fortress. Good footwear is advisable in the damp sloping tunnels, and although some are open and illuminated, a flashlight is handy in the others. In the **Almacén de Pólvora** (gunpowder store), there is a reproduction of Admiral Vernon's map, dating from his abortive attempt to take the city in 1741. A statue of Don Blas de Lezo below the fortress has a plaque displaying the medal prematurely struck celebrating Vernon's 'victory'.

Convento La Popa
Daily 0830-1730, US$1.50, children and students US$1, guides available. Walking up on your own is not recommended; either take a guided tour or take a public bus to Teatro Miramar at the foot of the hill (US$0.75), then bargain for a taxi up (they will try to charge around US$20, including waiting time.

Further east on the Cerro de la Popa, nearly 150 m high, the Convento La Popa has a fine view of the harbour and city. The complex includes the Augustinian church and monastery of Santa Cruz (Convento La Popa) and the restored ruins of the convent dating from 1608. In the church is a beautiful image of the Virgin of La Candelaria, with a golden crown, reputed to be a deliverer from plague and a protector against pirates. The statue was blessed by the Pope on his visit in 1986. The Virgin's day is 2 February and for nine days before the feast thousands of people go up the hill by car, on foot, or on horseback, carrying lighted candles on the feast day itself. There is an attractive bougainvillea-covered cloister with a well in the centre, and a museum with illuminated manuscripts, old maps, music books, relics and an image of the *Cabro de Oro* (golden goat) found by the Augustinians on the site, presumed to be an object of veneration of the indigenous people who previously inhabited the area. The name was bestowed on the hill because of its imagined likeness to a ship's poop deck.

Beaches and islands
an unmissable part of the Cartagena experience

Cartagena is surrounded on almost all sides by water and travellers will be drawn to the city's sparkling Caribbean beaches.

Bocagrande
To get to Bocagrande, take a bus south from the Puerta del Reloj, taxi US$2.50, or walk.

Just under a kilometre from the old city, along a seafront boulevard, Bocagrande is a spit of land crowded with hotel and apartment towers. Thousands of visitors flock to the beach with its accompanying resort atmosphere, fast-food outlets, shops – and dirty sea water. The water quality improves if you go as far as the **Hilton** ① *www.cartagena.hilton.com*, an excellent hotel at the end of the peninsula. **Fuerte Castillo Grande** on the tip of Bocagrande was built to protect the inner harbour of Cartagena, along with **Fuerte San José de Manzanillo** on the mainland. Access to Castillo Grande itself is restricted, but there is a very good view of the harbour, cruise boats and port activity from the end of Calle 6/Carrera 14, Bocagrande: in the centre of the harbour is a statue of the Virgin, with the port installations of Manga Island visible on the other side of the bay.

Marbella and the northern beaches
Marbella beach is just north of Las Bóvedas. This is the locals' beach and therefore quieter than Bocagrande during the week and good for swimming, though subject at times to dangerous currents. Beyond Marbella and the airport, the promontory is built up with high rises, including many well-known hotels which have their own access to the beach. City buses run to Los Morros and Las Américas conference centre, carrying on towards La Boquilla. Further north still, **Playa Manzanillo** is a sparsely populated stretch of beach, great for those looking

to get away from the crowds but still stay close to the city. There are also plenty of upscale dining options near the turn-off to Manzanillo.

Isla de Tierrabomba and Bocachica

The island of Tierrabomba lies between Bocagrande and Barú Island, forming a natural barrier between the Bahía de Cartagena and the Caribbean. The passage into the bay, known as Bocachica, is overlooked by the fortress of **San Fernando** at the southern tip of Tierrabomba and by **Fuerte San José**, opposite on Barú. The two forts were once linked by heavy chains to prevent surprise attacks by pirates. Like Bocagrande, **Bocachica beach** on Tierrabomba isn't very clean and you may be hassled here too.

Boats leave for Tierrabomba from a two-storey glass building halfway along the Muelle Turístico, which also has some tourist information. The round trip can take up to two hours each way and costs about US$5 with the regular service, more with private boats. Boats taking in Bocachica and the San Fernando fortress include *Alcatraz*, which runs a daily trip. Alternatively, you can cross from Bocagrande; *lanchas* leave from near the Hilton hotel and go to **Punta Arena beach** on Tierrabomba.

Isla Barú

Barú is a long thin island, with mostly fine white-sand beaches, separated from the mainland only by the **Canal del Dique**. The stopping place for tourist boats from Cartagena is **Playa Blanca**, which is crowded in the mornings but peaceful after the tour boats have left at around 1400. There are several fish restaurants on the beach, a growing number of upmarket places to stay and a few hammock and camping places. Take repellent against sandflies if sleeping in a tent or *cabaña*, and bring food and water since these are expensive on Barú. There have been reports of people drinking alcohol and then renting jet skis at Playa Blanca; keep your wits about you when swimming or snorkelling, as safety measures aren't always complied with.

There are various ways of getting to Playa Blanca. The most common is to take a bus from the centre to **Pasacaballo**, US$0.60 and then cross over the Canal del Dique via a five-minute ferry, US$0.50. There is also a bridge which allows for direct trips via taxi, or visitors can take a motortaxi via **Santa Ana** (45 minutes). Alternatively, fast boats to Playa Blanca leave **Bazurto** market, near La Popa, 0700-0930 daily, US$15 one way; public boats cost US$5. There are also touristy, expensive boats from the tourist dock (Muelle Turístico) at 0830 which stop at Playa Blanca as part of a tour, US$20-32. There is a 'port tax' of US$4.50 payable at the entrance to the muelle or on the boat. Neither the area nor the boats are particularly safe and boatmen can be persistent; be sure to pay the captain and not his 'helpers' and arrange a return pick-up time. There are also boats from the tourist dock which may stop at Playa Blanca as part of a tour to the Islas del Rosario (see below). When taking boat trips be certain that you and the operator understand what you are paying for. You can arrange to be left and collected later, or you can try to catch an earlier boat on to Islas del Rosario or back to Cartagena after passengers have been dropped off at the beach.

choose mangroves and mud baths or beaches and coral reefs

Ciénaga la Caimanera

To the northeast, the coastline is characterized by *ciénagas* (mangrove swamps). At La Boquilla canoe trips can be made to explore the Ciénaga la Caimanera, a labyrinth of mangroves full of wildlife (motorboats are not allowed). Local guides cost US$15 per person, and they will catch oysters for you to eat. Further north near **Galerazamba** is the clay bath of **Volcán del Totumo** ⓘ *entry to the cone US$3.50, mud bath US$3.50, massage available for a small extra fee*. Climb up steep steps to the lip of the 20-m-high crater and slip into the grey cauldron of mud, which is a comfortable temperature. The crater is about 10 m across and reputed to be over 500 m deep. You wash off in the nearby *ciénaga*, in beautiful surroundings.

To get there, catch a bus from Cartagena bus terminal to the turn-off (US$2, 45 km), then take a mototaxi to the crater (US$1, 10 minutes). Taking a tour from Cartagena may cost more but will save a lot of time. Tours to the volcano last about six hours and cost from US$20 depending on what is included (with or without lunch, trip to Manzanillo beach, etc). This has become a very popular excursion and the bath may be very busy.

Islas del Rosario

The Islas del Rosario are part of the Parque Nacional Natural Corales del Rosario y San Bernardo, which includes the long island of Barú to its furthest tip (see page 37) and the Islas de San Bernardo (see page 59).

These picture-postcard coral islands, 45 km southwest of the Bay of Cartagena, are low lying and densely vegetated, with narrow strips of fine sand. **Isla Grande** is the largest and best conserved, with a profusion of aquatic and avian life. The island has access to some of the best coral reefs in the archipelago and diving and snorkelling are available. Isla Grande and some of the smaller islets are easily accessible for day trippers and those who wish to stay in one of the hotels. Other visitors who may need permits (US$2.55 entrance fee, park open 0800-1700) should contact the national parks office in Bogotá (see page 131) or **Ecohotel La Cocotera** ⓘ *T316-474 0871, www.ecohotellacocotera.com*. Day trips usually include a stop at the **Oceanario San Martín de Pajarales** ⓘ *US$9, note that the price of entry to the aquarium is not included in boat fares (check if open before setting out)*, and time at Playa Blanca on Isla Barú (see page 37).

Travel agencies and the hotels offer excursions from the **Muelle Turístico** in Cartagena, leaving 0700-0900 and returning 1530-1730, costing from around US$20 (free if staying at one of the hotels), lunch included; book in advance. Overnight trips can be arranged through agencies, but they are overpriced. Note that in addition to the tour and the national park fee (US$3), there is an additional 'port tax' of US$4.50 payable at the entrance to the muelle or on the boat. For the cheapest rates, buy tickets direct from the boat owners (make sure they are the boat owners!) at the dockside. Groups of five or more people should try hiring their own boat for the day and bargaining for a fair price. This way you get to see what you want in the time available, rather than dodging the beach vendors around the tour boats. If you wish to enjoy the islands at your leisure there are several hotels (see Where to stay, page 42).

Tourist information

Useful websites include
www.ticartagena.com and
www.cartagenacaribe.com.

Corporación Turismo Cartagena de Indias (Corpoturismo)
Casa del Marqués del Premio Real,
Pl de la Aduana, T5-660 1583,
www.cartagenadeindias.travel.
Daily Mon-Sat 0900-1200, 1300-1800,
Sun and holidays 0900-1700.
This is the main tourist office and has
very helpful and knowledgeable staff.

There are also kiosks in Plaza de la Paz
(same hours as above), at the airport
(daily 0700-2300, reduced hours on Sun),
Bocagrande, Av del Malecón, opposite
Parque Flanagan (Mon-Sat 0800-1200,
1300-1700, Sun 0900-1700) and at
the Sociedad Portuaria Regional de
Cartagena (open for cruise ship arrivals).

Instituto Agustín Codazzi
C 34, No 3A-31, Edif Inurbe, www.igac.
gov.co. Mon-Fri 0730-1545.
Contact for maps.

Instituto de Patrimonio y Cultura de Cartagena
C Larga No 9A-47, T5-664 9443,
www.ipcc.gov.co.
May also provide information.

Where to stay

Hotel prices rise for the high seasons,
Nov-Mar and Jun-Jul. From 15 Dec to
31 Jan they can increase by as much
as 50% (dates are not fixed and vary at
each hotel). Hotels tend to be heavily
booked right through to Mar. Bargain
in low season.

Historic centre
There is a growing number of attractive
boutique hotels in Cartagena. Most
budget hostels are in Getsemaní. This
area is very popular with travellers and
has been smartened up, with many
places to stay, eat and drink (lots of
happy hour offers). Do not, however,
walk alone late at night.

See the description of the Historic
centre for descriptions and websites
of colonial buildings converted to
luxury hotels: **Charleston Santa Teresa**
(see page 31), **Casa de Pestagua** (see
page 34), **San Agustín** (see page 34)
and **Santa Clara** (see page 34) are all
special places to stay.

$$$$ Agua
C de Ayos, No 4-29, T5-664 9479,
www.hotelagua.com.co.
Exclusive, pricey, small boutique hotel,
colonial, quiet, pleasant patio.

$$$$ Cartagena de Indias
C Vélez Daníes 33, No 4-39, T5-660 0133,
www.movichhotels.com.
Small hotel in a colonial building,
comfortable, luxury accommodation
with pool and terrace with great view
of the city.

$$$$ El Marqués
C Nuestra Señora del Carmen,
No 33-41, T5-664 4438, www.
elmarqueshotelboutique.com.
A house belonging to the Pestagua
family, famous in the 1970s for its
celebrity guests. The central courtyard
has giant birdcages, hanging bells and
large palm trees. The rooms are crisp
and white. Peruvian restaurant, wine
cellar and a spa. Exquisite.

$$$$ La Passion
C Estanco del Tabaco, No 35-81, T5-664 8605, www.lapassionhotel.com.
Moroccan-style chic, elegant and discreet comfort, helpful staff, breakfast served by the roof top pool, very pleasant. Some rooms have balconies. Massage treatments and boat trips to Islas del Rosario organized. Highly recommended.

$$$$-$$$ Casa La Fe
Parque Fernández de Madrid, C 2a de Badillo, No 36-125, T5-664 0306, http://kalihotels.com.
Discreet sign (pink building), run by British/Colombian team. Very pleasant converted colonial house, quiet, jacuzzi on roof, free bicycle use. Recommended.

$$$ Hostal Casa Baluarte
C Media Luna, No 10-86, Getsemaní, T5-664 2208, www.hostalcasabaluarte.com.
Small rooms in colonial house, family-run, fan, laundry service. Offers massage and can arrange tours to the Islas del Rosario.

$$$ Kartaxa LifeStyle
C de las Bóvedas, No 39-120, T5-645 5300, http://hotelkartaxacartagena.com.
Near the delightful Plaza San Diego, this colonial building has modern rooms with an art and literature theme, courtyard, **La Comunión** restaurant.

$$$ Las Tres Banderas
C Cochera de Hobo, No 38-66, T5-660 0160, www.hotel3banderas.com.
Off Plaza San Diego, popular, helpful owner, very pleasant, safe, quiet, good beds, spacious rooms, massage treatments, small patio. Price depends on standard of room and season. Free ferry transport to sister hotel on Isla de la Bomba, has another hotel in Manzanillo.

$$$ Monterrey
Paseo de los Mártires Cra 8B, No 25-103, T5-650 3030, www.hotelmonterrey.com.co.
Colonial style, nice terrace with jacuzzi, pool, business centre, comfortable rooms.

$$ Hostal Santo Domingo
C Santo Domingo, No 33-46, T5-664 2268, hsantodomingopiret@yahoo.es.
Prime location, rooms are simple and open onto a sunny patio. Gate is usually locked, so security is good.

$$-$ Mamallena
C de la Media Luna, No 10-47, T5-670 0499, www.hostel mamallenacartagena.com.
Rooms and dorms (US$12, some a/c), in same group as Mamallena hostels in Panama, www.mamallena.com. Thorough info on boat travel to Panama and on local activities and day tours. There's a small kitchen, café, breakfast, tea and coffee included.

$$-$ Marlin
C de la Media Luna, No 10-35, T5-664 3507, www.hotelmarlin cartagena.com.
Aquatic-themed hostel run by a friendly Colombian. Private rooms and dorms (US$10 pp). Has a fine balcony overlooking the busy C de la Media Luna, free coffee, laundry service, lockers, tours and bus tickets organized. Recommended.

$ El Viajero Hostel Cartagena
C Siete Infantes, No 9-45, T5-660 2598, www.hostelcartagena.com.
Member of the South American chain of hostels, with a/c in rooms and dorms (average dorm bed price US$13-15 pp), busy and popular party hostel with bar, daily activities including dance lessons.

$$-$ Villa Colonial
C de las Maravillas, No 30-60, Getsemaní,
T5-664 5421, www.hotelvillacolonial.com.
Safe, well-kept hostel run by friendly
family, English spoken, cheaper with
fan, tours to Islas del Rosario. Its sister
hotel, **Casa Villa Colonial**, C de la Media
Luna No 10-89, same phone, www.
casavillacolonial.com, is more upmarket
(**$$**) and is also recommended.

$ Casa Viena
C San Andrés, No 30-53 Getsemaní,
T5-668 5048, T320-538 3619,
www.casaviena.com.
Popular traveller hostel with very
helpful staff who provide lots of
information and sell tours and
Brasilia bus tickets. Cooking facilities,
washing machine, TV room, range of
dorms (US$9-10.25) and rooms: more
expensive with private bath. Enquire
here for information about boats
to Panama.

$ Familiar
C El Guerrero, No 29-66, Getsemaní,
T5-664 2464, www.hosteltrail.com/
hostels/hotelfamiliar.
Fresh and bright, family-run hotel
with rooms set around a colonnaded
patio. Has a good noticeboard full of
information. Recommended.

$ Hostal Casa Nativa
C Tumbamuertos, No 38-68, T5-645
6064, www.nativahostal.com.
No frills hostal ideally located in the
centre. Dorms for 4 to 8 people, no
private rooms. A decent budget option.

Bocagrande

$$$$ Capilla del Mar
Cra 1, No 8-12, T5-650 1500,
www.capilladelmar.com.

Resort hotel across the road from
the beach, with swimming pool
on the top floor and 2 restaurants
featuring regional cuisine.

$$$$-$$$ Cartagena Millennium
Av San Martín, No 7-135, T5-642
4747 ext 2, www.hotelcartagena
millennium.com.
A range of different suites and spacious
rooms at various prices. Chic and
trendy, with minimalist decor, a small
pool, restaurant serving typical and
international food, a terrace bar and
a lobby bar, good service.

$$$$-$$$ Hotel Caribe by Faranda
Cra 1, No 2-87, T5-650 1160,
www.hotelcaribe.com.
Enormous Caribbean-style hotel, the first
to be built in Cartagena, retaining some
splendour of bygone years, with 2 newer
annexes, a/c, beautiful grounds and a
swimming pool. Expensive restaurant,
has several bars overlooking the sea,
various tour agencies and a dive shop.

$$$$-$$$ Playa Club
Av San Martín, No 4-87, T5-665 0552,
www.hotelplayaclubcartagena.com.
Good rooms, inviting pool and direct
access to the beach. TV, a/c and breakfast
included. Restaurant on premises.

$$$ Bahía
Cra 4 with C 4, T5-665 0316,
www.hotelbahiacartagena.com.
Retains the feel of a 1950s hotel – it
was opened in 1958 – but with mod
cons such as Wi-Fi and safes in rooms.
Discreet and quiet, with a fine pool
and restaurant.

$$$-$$ Charlotte
Av San Martín, No 7-126, T5-642 4744
ext 2, www.hotelescharlotte.com.

Comfortable rooms stylishly designed in cool whites. Has a small pool, and Wi-Fi by the pool. Smart restaurant serving regional food. Recommended.

$$ Mary
Cra 3, No 6-53.
Basic rooms but pleasant and friendly. A/c or fan.

Marbella and the northern beaches

$$$-$$ Hotel Kohsamui
Anillo Vial, Entrada Km 9.7 a Manzanillo del Mar, T317-648 9303, www.kohsamuicartagena.com.
Situated 20 km north of Cartagena, this is an ideal spot for relaxation and rejuvenation. Owner María Fernanda runs the hotel and has information on mangrove tours, excursions and trips to Islas del Rosario and Volcán del Totumo. Amenities include a/c and fans, security box, Wi-Fi, minibar, restaurant, spa with massage, and a 2nd-floor terrace with hammocks. 10% discount for paying in advance. Highly recommended.

Isla Barú

$$$ Playa Manglares
Km 12, Isla Barú Ararca, T317-657 1315, www.playamanglares.com.
Ecolodge, B&B, owned and run by Olga Paulhiac, organic food, yoga available, evening cocktails, attentive service, delightful.

$$ Hostal Restaurante Mama Ruth
Isla Barú, T300-710 2444, Mamaruthbaru@gmail.com, see Facebook.
Thatched cabins right on the beach and a popular restaurant. Recommended.

Islas del Rosario

$$$$ San Pedro de Majagua
Isla Grande; book at C del Torno, No 39-29, Cartagena, T5-693 0987, www.hotelmajagua.com.
Everything from a 'pillow menu' to Egyptian cotton bed sheets, this is a lovely, luxurious place for utter relaxation.

$$$$-$$$ Isla del Pirata
C 6, No 2-26, local 2, Edif Granada, Bocagrande, T5-665 2952, www.hotelislapirata.com.
Simple, comfortable *cabañas*, activities include diving, snorkelling, canoeing and pétanque, good Caribbean restaurant. Prices include transport to the island, food and non-guided activities. Highly recommended.

$$$ Ecohotel La Cocotera
Comunidad de Orika, Isla Grande, www.ecohotellacocotera.com.
Rooms with bath and solar power, also has camping and hammocks, restaurant, diving school.

Restaurants

There is a wide range of excellent restaurants. Reservations are recommended during high season. At cafés try *patacón*, a round flat 'cake' made of green banana, mashed and baked; it's also available from street stalls in Parque del Centenario in the early morning. At restaurants ask for *sancocho*, the local soup of the day made from vegetables and fish or meat. Stands serving tasty shrimp cocktails can be found just outside of El Centro. Also try *obleas* for a snack: biscuits with jam, cream cheese or caramel fudge (*arequipe*); and *buñuelos*, deep-fried cheese dough balls. Fruit juices are fresh, tasty and cheap in Cartagena: a good place is on the Paseo de los Pegasos (Av Blas de Lezo) from the many stalls alongside the boats. **Crepes y Waffles**, **Jeno's Pizza** and **Juan Valdez** have outlets in the centre, Bocagrande and elsewhere.

Historic centre

$$$-$$ Donde Olano
C Santo Domingo, No 33-81, T5-664 7099, www.dondeolano.com.
Tucked away, Art Deco style, intimate atmosphere, great seafood with French and Creole influences.

$$ Bistro
C de los Ayos, No 4-46, T5-660 2065, www.el-bistro.com. Closed Sun.
German-run restaurant with a relaxed atmosphere. Sofas, music, Colombian and European menu at reasonable prices, German bakery. Recommended.

$$ Café Zebra
Plaza San Diego, No 8-34.
Café with a wide selection of coffees, hot sandwiches and African dishes.

$$ El Balcón de San Diego
C de Tumbamuertos, No 38-85, p 2 (above Zebra), T5-643 4393.
Small restaurant with a nice balcony overlooking the Plaza de San Diego. Good atmosphere and good views.

$$ Juan del Mar
Plaza San Diego, No 8-12, T5-664 2782, www.juandelmar.com.
Two restaurants in one: inside for expensive seafood, outside for fine, thin-crust pizzas, though you are likely to be harassed by street hawkers, as with any place on the street here.

$$ Lunarossa
C Media Luna No 9-91 y San Andrés.
Italian place, with pastas, thin-crust pizzas and other dishes, also has a cocktail bar.

$$ Oh! La La
C de los Ayos, No 4-48, T5-660 1757, see Facebook.
Café/restaurant serving good French and Colombian food. Next door are **Jugoso** juice bar and **El Gallinero** for ice creams, yoghurts and snacks.

$$ Perú Fusión
C de los Ayos, No 4-36, T5-660 5243, see Facebook.
Good value Peruvian-style food, including ceviches.

$$ Teriyaki
Plaza San Diego, No 8-28, T5-664 8651, www.teriyaki.com.co.
Serves sushi and Thai food in smart surroundings.

$$-$ Casa Suiza
C de la Soledad, No 5-38.
For breakfast, lunch such as lasagne, salads, cheeses dishes, also does take-away, Wi-Fi.

$$-$ La Casa de Socorro
C Larga, No 8B-112, Getsemaní, T315-718 6666.
Busy at lunchtime, serves seafood and Caribbean dishes. There are 2 restaurants of the same name on the street and this is the original.

$$-$ La Cocina de Pepina
C Vargas, No 9A-6, T5-664 2944.
Serving Colombian-Caribbean fare, established by well-known chef and cookbook author María Josefina Yances Guerra, who passed away in 2014.

$ El Coroncoro
C Tripita y Media, No 31-22.
Typical restaurant which is popular
at lunchtime and serves good food.

$ Este es el punto
C San Andrés, No 30-35.
Another popular restaurant,
comida corriente at lunchtime,
also serves breakfast.

$ La Esquina del Pan de Bono
*San Agustín Chiquito, No 35-78,
opposite Plazoleta San Agustín.*
Breads, *empanadas*, *pasteles* and
juices, popular for a quick snack.

$ La Mulata
C Quero, No 9-58.
A popular lunchtime venue with locals,
you get a selection of set menu dishes.
Try the excellent seafood casserole and
coconut lemonade. Wi-Fi.

$ Pizza en el Parque
C 2a de Badillo, No 36-153.
This small restaurant serves delicious
pizzas with some interesting flavours
(pear and apple) which you can enjoy
in the delightful atmosphere of Parque
Fernández de Madrid.

East of the historic centre

$$$ Club de Pesca
*San Sebastián de Pastelillo fort,
Manga island, T5-651 7400,
www.clubdepesca.com.*
Wonderful setting, excellent fish
and seafood. Recommended.

Bocagrande

$$$ Ranchería's
Av 1A, No 8-86. T5-665 6163
Serves mainly parrilla-style meats in
thatched huts just off the beach.

$$$-$$ Arabe
*Cra 3A, No 8-83, T5-665 4365, www.
restaurantearabeinternacional.com.*
Upmarket Arab restaurant serving
tagines, etc. A/c, indoor seating or
pleasant outdoor garden.

$$$-$$ Carbón de Palo
Av San Martín, No 6-40, T5-665 6004.
Steak heaven (and other dishes),
cooked on an outdoor *parrilla*.

$ La Fonda Antioqueña
Cra 2, No 6-164, T5-665 5805.
Traditional Colombian food
from Antioquia served in a
pleasant atmosphere.

Marbella and the northern beaches
There are good fish dishes in La Boquilla
and upscale dining options (including
a gourmet supermarket) at the turn-off
to Manzanillo.

$$ Archie's Trattoria
*Km 9 via Manzanillo, Local 601,
T5-643 7070, www.archies.co.*
Chain Italian restaurant serving delicious
thin-crust pizzas and a large selection
of pastas.

$$ Hotel Kohsamui
*Trans 2, No 3-51, Manzanillo,
T317-648 9303.*
Chef Elbert runs the restaurant in the
hotel, serving up a variety of seafood
dishes, including fresh ceviches, *arroz
con mariscos* and fried fish. Probably
the best seafood on the beach.

Bars and clubs

Most night life is found in the historic
centre. Many of the hotels have
evening entertainment and can
arrange *chiva* tours, usually with free
drinks and live music on the bus.

Most places don't get going until after 2400, though the Cuban bars **Donde Fidel** (Portal de los Dulces), and **Café Havana** (see below) start a bit earlier and are recommended for Cuban salsa. The former is open daytime, with good atmosphere. Many clubs are on C del Arsenal. Most bars play crossover music.

Historic centre

Café del Mar
Baluarte de Santo Domingo, El Centro.
The place to go for a drink at sundown.

Café Havana
C de la Media Luna y C del Guerrero, T314-556 3905, www.cafehavana cartagena.com. Wed-Sat 2030-0400.
A fantastic Cuban bar/restaurant, which feels like it has been transported from Havana brick by brick. The walls are festooned with black-and-white portraits of Cuban salsa stars and live bands play most nights. No credit cards. Highly recommended.

Quiebra Canto
Cra 8B, No 25-119 at Parque Centenario, next to Hotel Monterrey and above Café Bar Caponero, Getsemaní, www.quiebracanto.com.
Good for salsa, nice atmosphere, free admission.

Tu Candela
Portal de los Dulces, No 32-25, www.tucandela.co.
Where you can dance to 'crossover' in the vaults, open 2000-0400.

Bocagrande
There are good local nightclubs in Bocagrande eg **La Escollera**, Cra 1, next to El Pueblito shopping centre, with other places nearby, including spontaneous musical groups on or near the beach most evenings.

Entertainment

Cinema
There are many cinemas in Cartagena. In Bocagrande there is one in the **Centro Comercial Bocagrande** (Cra 2, No 8-142, T5-665 5024). Others are in the **Centro Comercial Paseo de la Castellana** (C 30, No 30-31, www. paseodelacastellana.com), and in **Centro Comercial La Plazuela** (Diag 31, No 71-130, www.multicentrolaplazuela.com).

Dance
El Colegio del Cuerpo, *Campus Universidad Jorge Tadeo Lozano, Módulo 6, Km 15-200, Anillo Vial Zona Norte, T5-665 4081, www.elcolegiodel cuerpo.org.* A classical dance studio that works with children from Cartagena's slums. They perform internationally and occasionally in Cartagena.

Festivals

Mid-Jan Festival Internacional de Música, www.cartagenamusicfestival. com. Classical music festival with associated education programme for young musicians.
End-Jan Hay Festival Cartagena, www.hayfestival.com. Franchise of the famous UK literary festival, with internationally renowned writers.
Jan-Feb La Candelaria, religious processions and horse parades (see La Popa, page 35).
Early Mar International Film Festival, www.ficcifestival.com. The longest running festival of its kind in Latin America. Although mainly Spanish American films are featured, the US,

Canada and European countries are represented in the week-long showings.

1 Jun Foundation of Cartagena, celebrations to commemorate the founding of the city.

End-Oct Cartagena de Indias Jazz Fest, www.jazzcartagena.es.

2nd week of Nov Independence celebrations: masked people in fancy dress dance to the sound of *maracas* and drums. There are beauty contests, battles of flowers and general mayhem.

Shopping

Pricey antiques can be bought in C Santo Domingo and there are a number of jewellery shops near Plaza de Bolívar in Centro, which specialize in emeralds. The handicraft shops in the Plaza de las Bóvedas (see page 35) have the best selection in town but tend to be expensive – cruise ship passengers are brought here. Woollen *blusas* are good value; try the **Tropicano** in Pierino Gallo building in Bocagrande. Also in this building are reputable jewellery shops.

Abaco, *C de la Iglesia with C Mantilla, No 3-86, T5-664 8338, www.abacolibros. com*. A bookshop and popular hangout for local writers and poets. Delightful atmosphere and a café serving juices and snacks.

Centro Comercial Getsemaní, *C Larga between San Juan and Plaza de la Independencia*. A large shopping centre. Good *artesanías* in the grounds of the convent.

El Centavo Menos, *C Román, No 5-08, Plaza de la Proclamación*. Good selection of Colombian handicrafts.

Exito, *Escallón y del Boquete*. A supermarket, with a/c and cafeteria.

Galería Cano, *Plaza Bolívar No 33-20, www.galeriacano.com.co (and at the* airport and Hotel Santa Clara). Has excellent reproductions of pre-Columbian designs.

H Stern, *Pierino Gallo shopping centre and at the Hilton Hotel*. Jewellery shop.

Librería Nacional, *C 2 de Badillo, No 36-27, T5-664 1448, www.librerianacional. com*. A good bookshop with large stock.

Upalema, *C San Juan de Dios, No 3-99*. A good selection of handicrafts.

Markets

The main market is to the southeast of the old city near La Popa off Av Pedro de Heredia (**Mercado Bazurto**). Good bargains in the **La Matuna** market, open daily including Sun.

What to do

City tours

Many agencies, hotels and hostels offer city tours, US$15-25, depending on length of tour and what's included etc. There are also hop-on, hop-off city sightseeing bus tours, www. citysightseeing.com.co and www. colombiatrolley.com. A party tour on a *chiva* bus costs US$20. **Horse-drawn carriages** can be hired for a trip around the walled city from Puerta del Reloj, about US$15-20 for up to 4 people. Or from opposite Hotel El Dorado, Av San Martín, in Bocagrande, to ride into town at night (romantic but a rather short ride). You can also rent **bicycles** for riding the city streets from several places in the historic centre.

Diving

Discounts are sometimes available if you book via the hotels. There is a recompression chamber at the naval hospital in Bocagrande.

Club Isla del Pirata, *Islas del Rosario, T5-665 5622, www.hotelislapirata.com*.

Has the best boats and is near the top end of the price range.

Diving Planet, *C Estanco del Aguardiente, No 5-09, T320-230 1515 (English and Portuguese), www.diving planet.org*. PADI training courses, PADI e-learning, snorkelling trips and various tours of the coral reefs and mangroves. English spoken.

Hotel Caribe, *Bocagrande (see Where to stay)*. Scuba lessons in its pool and diving at its resort on Isla Grande, US$130 and up.

La Tortuga Dive Shop, *Edif Marina del Rey, C 1, No 2-23, loc 4, Av del Retorno, El Laguito, Bocagrande, T5-665 6994, www.tortugadive.com*. Fast boat, which allows for trips to Isla Barú as well as Los Rosarios.

Yates Alcatraz, *Islas del Rosario*. Economical outfit; enquire at the quay.

Football
Estadio Jaime Morón León, *Villa Olímpica, south of the city*. Games are infrequent.

Language schools
Nueva Lengua School, *T315-855 9551, www.nuevalengua.com*. Offers courses ranging from ½-day schedules to a scheme that arranges volunteer jobs. There are even Spanish courses combined with dance, music, adventure, kitesurfing or diving.

Tour operators
Aventure Colombia, *C de la Factoría, No 36-04, T5-660 9721, www.aventure colombia.com*. Also with branches in Bogotá and Santa Marta. The only tour organizer of its kind in Cartagena, French/Colombian-run, offering alternative tours across Colombia, local and national activities and expeditions, working (wherever possible) with local and indigenous groups. The focus is on ecotourism and trekking, also organizes boat trips. Highly recommended.

Ocean & Land, *Cra 2, No 4-15, Edif Antillas, Bocagrande, T5-665 7772, 727, oceanlandtours_cartagena@hotmail.com*. Organizes city tours, rumbas in *chivas* (brightly coloured local buses) and other local activities.

Yachting
Club Isla del Pirata, *T5-665 5622, www.hotelislapirata.com*. Has the best boats and is near the top end of the price range; **Yates Alcatraz** is more economical; enquire at the quay.

Club Náutico, *Av Miramar No 19-50, Isla Manga (across the Puente Román), T5-660 4863, www.clubnauticocartagena. com*. Good for opportunities to charter, crew or for finding a lift to other parts of the Caribbean.

Transport

Air
Rafael Núñez Airport (www.sacsa.co) is 1.5 km from the city in the Crespo district and can be reached by local buses from Blas de Lezo, in the southwest corner of El Centro. A bus from the airport to Pl San Francisco costs US$0.60; a taxi to San Diego or the centre is US$3 and to Bocagrande, US$5.75, but drivers may charge more. City buses can be very crowded so if you have a lot of luggage, a taxi is recommended. There is a *casa de cambio* (daily 0830-2000) at the airport, but rates are better in town. Travel agents have offices on the upper level. There are also a number of fast-food outlets.

There are direct flights daily to/from major Colombian cities, **San Andrés** and smaller places in the north of the country, as well as direct international flights to/from Fort **Lauderdale**, **Miami**, **New York** and **Panama**. From Dec to Mar flights can be overbooked, so arrive at the airport early. Airline servicing the airport include **Avianca**, C del Arzobispado, No 34-52, T5-664 7376, Mon-Fri 0800-1200, 1400-1800, Sat 0800-1300; Av Venezuela 33, No 8B-05, Edif City Bank, loc B2, T5-664 7822; also in Bocagrande, C 7, No 7-17, L 7, T5-665 0287 and at the airport, T5-666 1175. **Copa**, at the airport, Mon-Fri 0800-1800, Sat-Sun 0800-1700. **EasyFly**, T5-693 0400. **LAN**, Cra 3, No 4 -21 local 1, T1-800 094 9490. **Viva Colombia**, T5-642 4989.

Bus

The bus terminal, known as the '**Terminal de Transportes**' (www.terminaldecartagena.com) is at least 35 mins away from town on the road to Barranquilla. A Metrocar city bus to the terminal from the centre costs US$0.65, or a taxi, US$5-7.50; agree your taxi fare before you get in.

Several bus companies run to **Barranquilla**, every 15 mins, 2-3 hrs, US$5-6; there's also a **Berlinastur** (www.berlinastur.com) minibus service from C 46C, no 3-80, Marbella,T5 693 0006 318-724 2424, and *colectivos* from C 70, Crespo, every 2 hrs (centre-to-centre service). To **Santa Marta**, hourly, US$13.50, 4 hrs. Few buses go direct to Santa Marta from Cartagena, most stop in Barranquilla. To/from **Bogotá** via Barranquilla and Bucaramanga, daily, 21-28 hrs (depending on number of checkpoints), US$34-37, several companies. To **Medellín** 665 km, US$41, more or less hourly from 0530, 13-16 hrs; book early (2 days in advance at holiday times); the road is paved but in poor

condition. To **Magangué** on the Río Magdalena (for connections to Mompós) with **Brasilia**, US$11-12, 4 hrs (www.expresobrasilia.com). To **Mompós**, direct bus with **Unitransco** or **Brasilia**, 0630, 8 hrs, US$40; **Toto Express**, T310-707 0838, totoexpress2@hotmail.com, runs a door-to-door *colectivo* service, 6-7 hrs, US$40. To **Riohacha**, US$18. To **Maicao** on Venezuelan border, in the evening, 8 hrs, US$24.

Car hire

Several of the bigger hotels have car rental offices in their foyers, such as **Bechs**, Hotel Bahía, Bocagrande, C 4 at Cra 4, local 1, T5-665 0318. There are also car rental companies in Edif Torremolinos, Av San Martín, including **International Car Rentals**, T5-665 5399, and **National**, T5-655 1215; and on Av San Martín: **Budget**, No 13-37 L-3, T5-664 1293; **Trans**, No 11-67, Edif Tulipana L-5, T5-665 2427. Multiple companies at the airport.

Sea

For boat services to Cartagena's beaches and islands, see pages 36-37. Boats also go from Cartagena to the **San Blas Islands** (Panama); the journey takes 5 days in total, 2 sailing to the archipelago and 3 touring the San Blas islands. Trips usually end at Porvenir on the mainland, from where you can continue to Colón and thence to Panama City. The fare, about US$550, includes food, water and snorkelling gear. Some boats are cheaper, but you get what you pay for, so take your time before choosing a boat. Some captains are irresponsible and unreliable. The journey is cramped so it's best to get on with the captain. There are many notices in hostels in Getsemaní advertising this trip, for example in **Casa Viena** and **Mamallena**. Also **Sailing Koala**, T312-670 7863, www.sailingkoala.com, which offers a trip to San Blas and Panama. If entering Panama by boat, tourists pay a US$105 immigration fee, although this isn't consistently applied.

Note On the street, do not be tempted by offers of jobs or passages on board a ship. Jobs should have full documentation from the Seamen's Union office and passages should only be bought at a recognized shipping agency.

Taxi
There are no meters; journeys are calculated by zones and fixed by the Alcaldía with fares ranging from US$2-3. It is quite common to ask other people waiting if they would like to share, but, in any case, always agree the fare with the driver before getting in. By arrangement, taxis will wait for you if visiting more remote places. Fares go up at night.

Caribbean
Colombia

Essential Caribbean Colombia

Finding your feet

Cartagena's **Rafael Núñez Airport** is served by direct daily flights to/from major Colombian cities and other smaller places in the north of the country, as well as by direct international flights to/from Lauderdale, Miami, New York and Panama City. From December to March flights can be overbooked, so turn up at the airport early. Santa Marta's **Simón Bolívar Airport** also gets very crowded in tourist season, when you will need to book flights well in advance. Barranquilla's **Ernesto Cortissoz Airport** is a cheaper and less busy alternative. There are also regional airports at Corozal (near Sincelejo), at Valledupar and Riohacha in the northeast and at Acandi in Darién. Daily buses run from Bogotá to Cartagena, Barranquilla and Santa Marta, and there are also very frequent services to/from Medellín.

Getting around

Boats are available all along the coast for trips to local beaches and offshore islands. A boat is also required for part of the journey to Mompós on the Río Magdalena. Most other destinations can be reached by bus or *colectivo*, although services are limited southwest of Monterría and are non-existent in the Darién and parts of the Península de la Guajira.

When to go

The climate on the Caribbean coast varies little during the year. Temperatures rise marginally between August and November when there is more frequent rain and there can be flooding. This area is relatively humid, but trade winds between December and February provide relief from the heat. Fiestas are taken seriously in this region, and if you want a quiet time you might want to avoid certain periods, especially between Christmas and Easter. If you want to join in, be sure to plan in advance or be prepared to struggle for accommodation and expect higher prices.

Time required

You'll need two to three weeks to visit Cartagena and Santa Marta, relax on the coast and explore the rainforest.

South of
Cartagena

A decade or so ago, the area south of Cartagena was a no-go zone. The road between Cartagena and Medellín was the scene of frequent kidnappings by guerrillas who would perform raids on passing traffic and quickly abscond into the region's network of densely vegetated hills. Today it's a different story and locals no longer sweat before making what was once a perilous journey. It is now even considered reasonably safe to travel between Cartagena and Medellín at night. That said, although towns such as Sincelejo and Montería are fine to pass through, we advise against staying there too long. Be warned, too, that drug smuggling is still very active in the area near the Panama border.

The improvement in security means that this area, rich in culture and natural wonders, has opened up to tourism. Southeast is the colonial town of Mompós (also spelt Mompox) stranded in a time warp on an island in the Río Magdalena. Due south of Cartagena is Tolú, gateway to the coral islands of San Bernardo (part of the Parque Nacional Natural Corales de Rosario y San Bernardo), while further along the coast is Arboletes, location of the largest mud volcano in the area. Further still is Turbo, a rough frontier town from where boats can be caught to the emerald green coastline of the Darién.

ON THE ROAD

Mud volcanoes

The Caribbean coast is peppered with several geological curiosities popularly known as 'mud volcanoes'. These large mud pools are believed to be the result of underground oil and gas deposits, which combine with water, forcing the mud to ooze to the surface. Often they form conical mounds, hence the name. Many of these pools can be found between the Gulf of Urabá and Santa Marta. Turbo has several in its proximity (Rodosalín, El Alto de Mulatos and Caucal), as does San Pedro de Urabá. The Volcán del Totumo is a popular day trip from Cartagena, but the pick of the bunch is Arboletes, where an enormous 30-m-wide lake has formed, a stone's throw from the beach.

Wallowing in the grey-black mud is a strange experience: it's impossible to sink, and attempts to swim are about as worthwhile as trying to battle your way across a vat of treacle. When you have had enough, clamber out and join the line of mud-caked figures waddling down to the Caribbean for a wash and a swim. The stuff is reportedly an excellent exfoliant and does wonders for the skin and hair.

Cartagena to Mompós

The highway towards Medellín goes southeast from Cartagena through **Turbaco**, 24 km, where there's a **botanical garden** ⓘ *1.5 km before the village on the left, www.jbgp.org.co, daily 0800-1600*. At **Malagana**, 60 km, the road splits; to reach Mompós continue east and then south towards **San Jacinto**, known for its *cumbia* music using *gaitas* and for its hand-woven hammocks, and **El Carmen de Bolívar**, 125 km. After another 40 km, a road runs east from the highway to **Magangué**, on the western loop of the Río Magdalena, the port for the savannas of Bolívar. From here boats go to La Bodega where you pick up the road again to reach the small town of Mompós.

Mompós

time-warp town in a unique riverine setting

The grand old Magdalena River splits in two just before Mompós. When the town was founded in 1540, Santa Cruz de Mompós was on the main branch of the river, and it became a major staging port for travellers and merchandise going to the interior. At the beginning of the 20th century, however, the river silted up with mud and became unnavigable for large boats, so traffic was diverted to the Braza de Lobo River. As a result, Mompós became a backwater, and it has remained practically untouched ever since.

Part of Mompós' charm lies in the fact that it is still quite difficult to reach and so retains much the same atmosphere you might have experienced had you visited in the early 20th century. In 1995 UNESCO declared it a World Heritage

Site for the quality of its colonial architecture and its fine churches. The town is also well known in Colombia for hand-worked gold and silver jewellery, especially filigree, as well as for its wicker rocking chairs. Today, in the evenings, as the sweltering heat begins to lessen and the bats start to swoop from the eaves of the whitewashed houses, locals carry their rocking chairs out onto the streets to chat with neighbours and watch the world go by.

Sights

The churches demonstrate the colonial origins of the town. **San Francisco** is probably the oldest, dating from the end of the 16th century, with an interesting interior. **Santa Bárbara**, on Calle 14 by the river, has a unique octagonal Moorish tower and balcony. Nearby on Calle 14, opposite Carrera 4, is a garden open to visitors (usually) with trees and flowering plants. **San Juan de Dios**, **La Concepción**, **Santo Domingo** and **San Agustín** are all worth visiting, but you may have to ask around for the key as they are normally only open during Mass. In the **Claustro de San Agustín** is a workshop where youngsters are taught local skills.

Mompós' rows of well-preserved buildings, some with balconies, have served as a backdrop in many Colombian films, including the adaptation of Gabriel

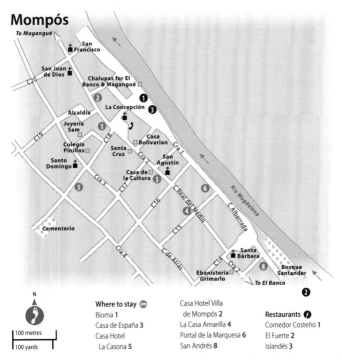

Mompós

To Maganguè

San Francisco

San Juan de Dios

Chalupas for El Banco & Maganguè ❶

La Concepción ❸

Alcaldía

Joyería Sam ❶

Casa Bolívarian

Colegio Pinillos

Santa Cruz

San Agustín

Santo Domingo

Casa de la Cultura ❸

❺

❻

Río Magdalena

C Albarrada

Cementerio

C Real del Medio

C16

C15

Santa Bárbara

Ebanistería Grimarlo

C de Atrás

C14

❽

Bosque Santander

To El Banco

❷

N

100 metres
100 yards

Where to stay 🛏
Bioma 1
Casa de España 3
Casa Hotel
  La Casona 5

Casa Hotel Villa
  de Mompós 2
La Casa Amarilla 4
Portal de la Marquesa 6
San Andrés 8

Restaurants 🍴
Comedor Costeño 1
El Fuerte 2
Islandés 3

García Márquez's *Chronicle of a Death Foretold* (1987). Among notable buildings are the **Casa de Gobierno**, once a home of the Jesuits and now the Alcaldía; the **Colegio Pinillos**, and the **Casa de la Cultura**, home of the local Academy of History. Facing the river on the Albarrada are the old customs house and the mansions of Spanish merchants, including the **Portales La Marquesa**.

The **cemetery** is of considerable historical interest; on one side of the central avenue lie the Conservatives; on the other, the Liberals. This political division of the town continued down Calle 18, running from the cemetery to the river. Try to visit the cemetery on the Wednesday of **Semana Santa** when it is illuminated by thousands of candles lit by the locals to honour the dead. There is also a popular jazz festival in October.

Mompós was particularly dear to Simón Bolívar, as it was the site of one of the greatest victories in his campaign to expel the Spanish from South America. "If to Caracas I owe my life, then to Mompós I owe my glory," he said (a monument outside the Alcaldía proclaims this). He stayed in what is now called the **Museo Cultural Casa Bolivariana** ① *C del Medio y 17, Mon-Fri 0900-1200, 1430-1700, Sat-Sun 0900-1300*, which houses memorabilia and some religious art exhibits.

Boat trips ① *3-4 hrs, US$10-15*, can be taken along the Río Magdalena and into the surrounding wetlands, which provide excellent opportunities for birdwatching. Alternatively take the small ferry across the river beyond the Parque Santander, US$0.50, and walk a little way up the track to where it meets another track. Turn sharp right and look for birds in the wet areas beyond the cattle pens; early morning or dusk are the best times. Beware of dogs. Ferocious mosquitoes and the odd bat are also a nuisance after dusk; take insect repellent and wear long sleeves.

Listings Mompós *map p55*

Where to stay

It is essential to book in advance for Semana Santa, the jazz festival and other holiday periods, when prices go up.

$$$-$$ Bioma
C Real del Medio (Cra 2), No 18-59, T5-685 6733, www.bioma.co.
Boutique style, cool and fresh, courtyard garden with running water, jacuzzi on roof terrace and a small pool. Rooms are large, family rooms have 2 floors. There's a restaurant but reserve in advance.

$$$-$$ La Casa Amarilla
Cra 1, No 13-59, T5-685 6326, www.lacasaamarillamompos.com.
A block up from the Iglesia Santa Bárbara near the riverfront. Master suites, suites and cheaper 'colonial' rooms, all beautifully decorated. All rooms open onto a cloister-style colonial garden. English owner Richard McColl is an excellent source of information on Colombia. Laundry, book exchange, use of kitchen, roof terrace, bicycle hire, tours arranged to silver filigree workshops and to wetlands for birdwatching and swimming (US$10 pp). Recommended.

$$$-$$ Portal de la Marquesa
Cra 1, No 15-27, on the Albarrada,
T315-343 1566, www.portaldela
marquesa.com.
New hotel in a converted colonial
mansion, fronting the river, with gardens
and patios, suites and standard rooms
with modern facilities, can arrange local
guides and boat trips.

$$ Casa de España
C Real del Medio (Cra 2),
No 17A-52, T5-685 5373, www.
hotelcasaespanamompox.com.
Some family rooms, a/c or fan, TV and
Wi-Fi. Snacks and drinks available.

$ Casa Hotel La Casona
C Real del Medio (Cra 2), No 18-58,
T5-685 5307, www.hotelmompos.com.
Fine colonial building with delightful
courtyards and plants, pool and
outdoor terrace.

$ Casa Hotel Villa de Mompox
Cra 2, No 14-108, 500 m east of
Parque Bolívar, T5-685 5208, http://
hotelvillademompox.blogspot.co.uk/.
Charming, family-run, decorated with
antique bric-a-brac. Also arranges rooms
for families during festivals.

$ San Andrés
C Real del Medio (Cra 2), No 18-23,
T5-685 5886, www.hotelsanandres
mompox.com.
Another fine, restored colonial building,
with nice sitting room and garden.
Rooms for 1-5 people, cheaper with fan,
on a corridor off the garden, spacious,
use of kitchen, meals extra. Same owner
as **Islandés** restaurant and tour company
(river tours).

Restaurants

Every night stallholders sell freshly
cooked food and fresh juices in
Plaza Santo Domingo.

$$$-$$ El Fuerte
Parque Santander, T314-564 0566,
www.fuertemompox.com.
Serves gourmet pizza in a restored
colonial building. It is the art gallery
of Walter Maria Gurth and displays his
wooden furniture. Contact in advance.

$ Comedor Costeño
On the riverfront between C 18 and C 19.
Good local food, popular for lunch.

$ Islandés
On the riverfront between C 18 and C 19.
In same vein as **Comedor Costeño** and
almost next door, same owner as **San
Andrés** (see Where to stay).

Shopping

Mompós is famous for its filigree gold
and silver jewellery and its wicker
rocking chairs. Several jewellers can be
found on C del Medio (Cra 2). You can
visit the workshops.

Jewellery
Filimompox, *C 23, No 3-23, T5-685 6604.*
Joyería Sam, *C 23 No 3-04, T311-403
5492.* Fine selection of beautifully
worked gold and silver earrings,
bracelets and brooches.
Santa Cruz, *Cra 2, No 201 132, T310-656
5568, tallersantacruz@yahoo.com.*

Transport

Cars are rare here: the main ways
to get around are bicycle, moped,
auto-rickshaw or walking.

Air The closest airport is **Corozal** (near Sincelejo), which has regular connections with **Medellín** and **Bogotá**. It's 1 hr by *colectivo* from Corozal Airport to Magangué, or 15 mins from Corozal to Sincelejo; then take a *colectivo* to Magangué, as below.

Bus Buses from Cartagena and Barranquilla travel to Mompós via Magangue for the river crossing (see below); buses from central Colombia travel via El Banco, while buses from Valledupar and Santa Marta travel via Bosconia. **Note** Prices for public transport rise Dec-Jan and at Easter.

Direct services to/from **Cartagena** are run by **Unitransco**, 8 hrs, US$20. **Toto Express**, T310-707 0838, totoexpress2@ hotmail.com, runs a door-to-door *colectivo*, 6-7 hrs, US$25. There are additional services between Cartagena and Magangué. **Omaira** runs a door-to-door *colectivo* service between Mompós and **Santa Marta**, 6 hrs, US$30, departs 0300 and 1100. From **Medellín**, Copetran runs an overnight service

from Medellín to Mompós, or catch the overnight **Rápido Ochoa or Brasilia** bus to Magangué, 12 hrs, US$41, or travel to Magangué by *colectivo* from **Sincelejo**, US$9.50, 1½ hrs. To **Valledupar** (via **Bosconia**), door-to-door service with local taxi/minibus driver Lalo Castro, T312-673 5226, US$20; if he isn't going, **CotraNorte**, **Cotracol** or **Cootracegua** buses daily, mornings only. From **Bogotá**, **Copetran** have a direct service at 1700, US$45, 14-15 hrs, otherwise **Copetran** and **Omega** have services to **El Banco** at 1700, 14 hrs, US$45, then take a 4WD to Mompós, US$9.50 (US$11 a/c), 1 hr.

Ferry To get to Mompós from Magangué you have to travel to **La Bodega**, either by fast *chalupa* (motorized canoe, 20 mins, US$2.50, life jacket provided), or on the vehicle ferry (from 0600, 1 hr, food and drink on board), which leaves from Yati, about 2 km outside town. From La Bodega you continue by *colectivo* to Mompós (1¼ hrs, US$6).

Coast south of Cartagena

beaches, islands and mud volcanoes

Tolú and around

Tolú, 35 km northwest of Sincelejo, on the coast, is a fast developing holiday town popular with Colombians and, increasingly, foreign tourists attracted by visits to the offshore islands and diving. Along the *malecón* (seafront promenade), there are plenty of bars and restaurants. A distinctive feature of the town is the number of bicycle rickshaws armed with loud sound-systems blasting out *vallenato*, salsa and reggaeton; the rickshaw drivers spend much of their time trying to outdo each other with the volume of their music.

There are also two mud volcanoes to visit in the area. The closest one is in **San Antero**, 30 minutes' drive from Tolú; a six-hour tour, including other sites of interest and lunch, costs US$55. The other is in San Bernando del Viento (see below). Trips to the mangrove lagoons are also recommended.

Islas de San Bernardo

Tolú is the main departure point for boat trips to the beautiful beaches of **Múcura Island** or **Tintipán** in the Islas de San Bernardo. The island beaches are of fine white sand and the water offshore is beautifully clear. There are a number of shacks serving seafood, including excellent barbecued lobster. Unfortunately, with several launches converging on the island at the same time, it can get crowded, and the number of beach vendors can detract from the beauty of the place. There is a charge for everything, including sitting at a table. To enjoy the islands at your leisure, it is better to stay overnight. It's also possible to reach the island from Cartagena, if you have a reservation at **Punta Faro** (one hour 45 minutes by boat, transfer included in the cost of accommodation).

Coveñas and around

There are, perhaps surprisingly, good beaches at **Coveñas**, 20 km further southwest, the terminal of the pipeline from the oilfields in the Venezuelan border area. Coveñas is essentially a 5-km-long stretch of road peppered with *cabañas* and hotels. During high season (Easter, Christmas to mid-January, June and July) it is very popular with Colombians eager to hit the beach and party. To get there, take a bus or *colectivo* from Tolú. Further along the coast, 18 km southwest of Coveñas, turn right at Lorica to reach **San Bernardo del Viento** from where launches can be arranged to **Isla Fuerte**, an unspoilt coral island with fine beaches and simple places to stay. It's a good place to dive, but there are very limited facilities on the island. Enquire at travel agencies in Cartagena and elsewhere for inclusive trips or negotiate in San Bernardo.

Arboletes

As well as being a convenient stopover on the way to Turbo and the Darién coast, the otherwise unremarkable town of Arboletes has one extraordinary attraction: the largest mud volcano in the area. The **Volcán de Lodo** is a 15-minute walk from town on the road to Montería or a two-minute taxi ride (US$7 return; the driver will wait for you while you bathe; mototaxi US$2). Dipping into this swimming pool-sized mud bath is a surreal experience – like swimming in treacle. It's very good for your skin. You can wash the mud off in the sea by walking to the beach 100 m below. There is a small restaurant and changing rooms (US$ 0.50), plus a locker room (US$1 per bag) and showers (US$0.50).

Turbo

At the mouth of the Gulf of Urabá is the port of Turbo: a hot, rough, frontier community with a lawless feel about it. It is a centre for banana cultivation. The beach is nice enough, although like everywhere on this stretch of the coast, the sea is a muddy brown due to its proximity to the gulf. There is little reason to stop here except to catch a boat to Capurganá and the Panamanian border.

Where to stay

Tolú

$$ Alcira
Av La Playa, No 21-151, T5-288 5016,
www.hotelalcira.amawebs.com.
Modern, on the promenade, with
restaurant and parking.

$ El Turista
Av La Playa, No 11-20, T5-288 5145.
The cheapest option in town and
good value for money. Next to all
the tour agencies.

$ Villa Babilla
C 20, No 3-40, Barrio el Cangrejo, T312-
677 1325, www.villababillahostel.com.
Run by a Colombian/German team.
3 blocks from the beach, well organized,
dorms and private rooms, good
restaurant, horse-riding, bike hire, good
information on diving and island tours.
Recommended travellers' hostel.

Islas San Bernardo

$$$$ Punta Faro
Isla Múcura, T317-435 9583,
www.puntafaro.com.
Low-key luxury resort with 45 rooms
in a gorgeous setting by the sea, inside
Corales del Rosario National Park.
Price includes all meals (buffet-style)
and happy hour cocktails. Return boat
transfer from Cartagena costs US$53
plus US$4.20 port tax (boats leave
once a day), some boats also leave from
Tolú. Massage treatments, hammocks
on the beach, eco walks around the
island and a good sustainability policy.
Highly recommended.

Coveñas and around
There are plenty of hotels in Coveñas,
many catering for family holidays.

$$$ Porto Alegre
Primera Ensenada, T315 282 8880,
www.hotelportoalegre.com.co.
Beachfront hotel, rooms for 2-5 people
or apartment for 8, with a/c, microwave,
pool, jacuzzi, breakfast included, no
restaurant but can arrange meals with
nearby establishments, similarly tours.

$$ pp Estado Natural Ecolodge
7 km from San Bernardo del Viento, T321-
724 7888, www.estado-natural.com.
Rustic cabins on a beach, compost toilets
and other sustainable practices, meals not
included but cabins have kitchen, activities
include birdwatching, windsurfing, trips
to Isla Fuerte, riding and guided tours.

$$ La Candelita
Primera Ensenada de Punta Piedra,
T314-561 6513.
Simple cabins for 2-6 people, with a/c or
fan, TV; principally a water sports centre,
including kitesurfing lessons and sailing.

Arboletes

$$$-$$ El Mirador
C Principal, T4-820 0441, www.
hotelelmiradordearboletes.com.
Self-styled 'boutique' hotel with
14 rooms, some with bunk beds ($ pp),
includes breakfast, restaurant and bar,
jacuzzi, internet and parking.

$ La Floresta
C Principal, T4-820 0034.
This small hotel has simple rooms
with private bathrooms and a/c.

Ask for a street-facing room if you want a window.

Turbo

$$ Castilla de Oro
C 100, No 14-07, T4-827 2185,
hotelcastilladeoro@hotmail.com.
The best option in town has a/c, safety box, minibar, a good restaurant and a swimming pool. Modern building with reliable water and electricity. Friendly staff.

$$ Simona del Mar
Km 13 Vía Turbo, T4-824 3729,
www.simonadelmar.com.
Turbo is not a safe place to walk around at night, so this option a few kilometres outside town is a safer choice. It has a number of *cabañas* in a tranquil setting near the beach. Good restaurant. A taxi to and from Turbo is US$10. You can also ask *colectivos* to drop you there.

Transport

Tolú
Tolú can be reached from Cartagena via **San Onofre**, or Toluviejo; continue from Toluviejo for 20 km to reach **Sincelejo**.

Bus Rápido Ochoa from **Cartagena** at 0615 and 0730, US$11. 7 a day to **Medellín** with Brasilia and Rápido Ochoa, US$36.50, via Montería except at night.

Turbo

Bus To **Medellín**, buses every 90 mins, 8-10 hrs, US$18-21. To **Montería**, Rápido Ochoa, 4-5 hrs, US$12. Fewer to **Cartagena**. Check safety carefully before travelling by road to/from Turbo.

Sea Turbo's port is known as El Waffe. Launches for **Capurganá**, T312-701 9839, leave daily at 0700-0900, 3 hrs, US$19. It's a spectacular journey that hugs the Caribbean shoreline of Darién. Rush for a seat at the back as the journey is bumpy and can be painful in seats at the front. There is a 10-kg limit on baggage (US$0.20 per extra kilo). Make sure that all your belongings, especially valuables, are in watertight bags and be prepared to get wet. From mid-Dec to end Feb the sea is very choppy and dangerous. We advise you not to make the journey at this time.

Darién Gap

blissful beaches backed by impenetrable jungle

The Darién Gap has long held a special place in travellers' lore as the ultimate adventure – and for good reason. This thin stretch of land, just 50 km wide and 160 km long, which links Central and South America, has some of the densest tropical jungle in the world – so dense that to date neither the Panamanians nor the Colombians have succeeded in building a road across it, and the only inland routes are by boat or on foot. At present, the Pan-American Highway, which stretches from Canada to Tierra del Fuego in Chile, stops at Yaviza in Panama, 60 km short of the frontier, and begins again 27 km west of Barranquillita, well into Colombia. The Darién is home to an incredible profusion of flora and fauna, as well as indigenous tribes who rarely see foreigners.

The trek across the Darién is held in high regard by adventurers but we strongly advise against it, not simply because it is easy (and fatal) to get lost, but also because bona fide travellers are not welcome (indigenous communities in Darién have never truly accepted trekkers passing through) and this area still has a heavy guerrilla presence. The Colombian government's successes against the FARC have pushed them to the extremes of the country, where they have come into conflict with those trafficking drugs from South to North America. Drug gangs find the density of the jungle a useful protection for running consignments and regard the area's infiltration by both FARC and ELN guerrilla groups as a threat to their land. As a result this has become a war zone, virtually deserted now by police and the military, and it is a hostile environment for any tourist. For the moment, only the foolhardy would attempt the land crossing. However, the Caribbean coastline, heavily patrolled by Colombian and Panamanian forces, is safe, though you should exercise caution if venturing into the forest beyond.

Acandí

Acandí is a small fishing village on the Caribbean side of the Darién. It has a spectacular, forest-fringed bay with turquoise waters. To the south are other bays and villages, such as **San Francisco**. From March to June, thousands of leatherback turtles come here to lay their eggs. There are several cheap *residencias* to stay in.

Capurganá

For many years, Capurganá and neighbouring Sapzurro (see below) have been among the best-kept secrets in Colombia. In this most isolated of Colombia's corners, a glistening, untouched shoreline of crystal waters and coral reefs backs onto quiet little villages where, at night, if you listen carefully, you can hear the howler monkeys calling to each other in the jungle-clad hills behind.

Capurganá has developed into a resort popular with affluent Colombians and is increasingly visited by foreigners, despite being somewhat difficult and expensive to get to. It is a quiet place: there are no banks or ATMs, nor are there any cars, just a couple of motorbikes. Taxi rides are provided by horse and carts, and someone has had the ingenious idea of attaching modified plastic seats.

There are two beaches in the village. **La Caleta** is at the northern end, beyond the pontoon, and is protected by a barrier reef, has golden sand and is the best for swimming. There are a couple of restaurants and several hotels and *cabañas* here. **Playa de los Pescadores**, south of the village, is fringed by palm and almond trees but has grey sand and is pebblier. Ask the fishermen about fishing trips from here in rowing boats.

Around Capurganá

Several half- and full-day trips can be made by launch to neighbouring beaches. **Aguacate** is a beautiful bay with clear, aquamarine water and a small beach. There is a rocky promontory with a blowhole and what locals call 'La Piscina', a natural jacuzzi amongst the rocks which you can lower yourself into using a rope. Aguacate has good snorkelling, but **Playa Soledad** is perhaps the most attractive beach in the area and was even used as the location for a Colombian reality TV programme. The beach has white sand and is fringed by palms. A return trip by launch boat costs US$15 per person, minimum five people. You can walk to Aguacate, 1½ hours along the coast, but not to Playa Soledad. Note that it can be difficult to obtain a return by launch if you walk.

A delightful half-day excursion is to **El Cielo** ⓘ *0600-1700, US$2; 40-min walk, take flip flops or waterproof boots for crossing a stream several times*, a small waterfall in the jungle. Take the path to the left of the airport and keep asking for directions. Just before the waterfall a small restaurant serves *patacones* and drinks. Alternatively, you can hire horses to take you there. Another horse-riding trip is to **El Valle de Los Ríos**, a valley in the jungle with several crystalline rivers and beautiful waterfalls (take a guide). The primary forest in this area is rich in wildlife; you might see, among other animals, sloths, howler monkeys, toucans, parrots, fishing eagles and several types of lizard and iguana.

There is excellent diving and snorkelling around Capurganá. You are likely to see nurse sharks, moray eels, spotted eagle rays, trumpetfish, jewfish, barracuda and hawksbill turtles, among other species, as well as large brain and elkhorn coral. Several of the hotels organize diving, but the independent dive centre **Dive and Green** (www.diveandgreen.com) is recommended.

Sapzurro

Reached by tours from Capurganá or by a beautiful four-hour hike along the coastline through jungle rich in wildlife, Sapzurro is a quiet little village in the Darién and the last outpost before Panama and Central America. Set in a shallow, horseshoe-shaped bay dotted with coral reefs, little happens in this village of less than 1000 inhabitants. There are no roads, let alone cars; the houses are linked by intersecting pathways bursting with tropical flowers. It has a couple of excellent little hostels and some good restaurants serving up home-cooked seafood. The bay offers superb snorkelling, with a couple of underwater caves to explore.

You can make a day trip to the small village of **La Miel** over the border in Panama by walking up the forested hill behind the village. There are breathtaking views of Panama and back into Sapzurro at the border on the brow of the hill. Be sure to take your passport; they won't stamp it for visits to La Miel, but they will take your details. This could qualify as the most relaxed border crossing in the world. The Colombian and Panamanian immigration officers share a hut and copy each other's notes.

La Miel has a gorgeous white-sand beach with beautiful, clear waters and a coral reef. The snorkelling is relatively good though a little low on fauna. There are a couple of shacks selling beer and food; try the sea snails in coconut sauce. You can arrange for a launch to pick you up and take you back to Sapzurro or Capurganá.

Colombian immigration Ask at the **Migración Colombia** office ⓘ *in Cartagena (see page 131), Medellín (C 19, No 80A-40 in Belén La Gloria section, T4-345 5500) or Montería (C 28, No 2-27, T4-781 0841, cf.monteria@migracioncolombia.gov.co, Mon-Fri 0800-1200, 1400-1700)*, whether the immigration office in Capurganá is open.

Entering Panama Panamanian immigration at Puerto Obaldía will check all baggage for drugs. Requirements for entry are proof of US$500 in the bank and a yellow fever certificate. There is a **Panamanian consul** ① *T310-303 5285, nayi051991@hotmail.com*, in Capurganá opposite the main square. Check with the consul in Cartagena, Medellín, or the embassy in **Bogotá** ① *C 92, No 7A-40, T01-257 5067, www.panamaenelexterior.gob.pa/bogota*, before setting out. However, these formalities are not required for day trips to Miel.

Listings Darién Gap

Where to stay

Capurganá

Accommodation and food are generally more expensive than in other parts of Colombia. Upmarket options include **Tacarcuna Lodge** (www.hotelesde costaacosta.com/capurgana) and **Bahía Lodge** (www.bahia-lodge.com).

$$ Cabaña Darius
T314-622 5638, www.darius capurgana.es.tl.
In the grounds of Playa de Capurganá, excellent value, simple, comfortable rooms in tropical gardens, fan, breakfast included.

$$ Marlin Hostal
Playa de los Pescadores, T310 593 6409, http://hostalmarlin.com/.
The best mid-range option in town, good rooms, also bunks ($), restaurant serving excellent fish.

$ Hostal Capurganá
C del Comercio, T316-482 3665, www.hostalcapurgana.net.
Comfortable, pleasant patio, well situated. Has a restaurant and offers tours. Price is per person for a 2-night, all-inclusive package, 3- and 4-nights also available; transfers from Turbo and Medellín can be included. Recommended.

$ Posada del Gecko
C del Comercio 2, T314-525 6037, www.posadadelgecko.com.
Small place, 5 rooms with bath and 3 cabins, gardens, popular café/bar that serves good Italian food. Also tours to San Blas Islands.

Sapzurro

$$ Paraíso Sapzurro
T313-685 9862, www.hosteltrail.com/ hostels/elchilenoresortparaiso.
Cabañas on the beach at the southern end of the village, Chilean-run (ask for El Chileno), higher price includes half-board. Also has dorms ($) and space for camping.

$ Zingara Cabañas
Camino La Miel, T313-673 3291, www. hospedajesapzurrozingara.com.
Almost the last building in Colombia, 2 lovely *cabañas* overlooking the bay. The owners have a vegetable and herb garden and sell home-made chutneys. This also doubles up as the village pharmacy.

Restaurants

Capurganá

$$ Donde Josefina
Playa La Caleta.
Josefina cooks exquisite seafood, served to you under a shady tree on the beach.

Try the lobster cooked in garlic and coconut sauce.

What to do

Capurganá
Diving
Dive and Green, *near the jetty, T311-578 4021, www.diveandgreen.com.* Dive centre offering PADI and NAUI, lots of courses, snorkelling and excursions to San Blas. English spoken.

Transport

Acandi
Air Daily flights to/from **Medellín** with **Aerolínea de Antioquia** (ADA, www.ada-aero.com), from US$90 and US$70 one way. These are twin Otter biplanes with just 16 passenger capacity, so be sure to book ahead.

Baggage limit of 10 kg; your baggage may have to follow on a later plane if it's seriously overweight.

Capurganá
Sea Launches to **Turbo**, 0800, US$19, 10 kg limit on baggage (US$0.25 per extra kg); we advise you not to make this journey from mid-Dec to end Feb. To **Acandí**, US$6. To **Sapzurro**, US$5, 30 mins. There are also launches to **Puerto Obaldía** in Panama, US$9. From here it's possible to catch an **Air Panamá** flight to **Panama City**, not daily, cost US$75-95, www.flyairpanama.com. Essential to book in advance.

Sapzurro
Sea Launch to **Capurganá**, US$5, 30 mins; to **Puerto Obaldía**, 45 mins, US$15.

Barranquilla
& around

Barranquilla, Colombia's fourth-largest city, lies on the western bank of the Río Magdalena, about 18 km from its mouth. It's a seaport (though less busy than Cartagena or Santa Marta), as well as a river port, and a modern industrial city with a polluted but colourful central area near the river. Many people stay a night in Barranquilla because they can find better flight deals than to Cartagena or Santa Marta. It's worth a short stay as the city is growing as a cultural centre, safety has improved and there are several things to do and see. It's also a good place to buy handicrafts, which are the same as can be found elsewhere but cheaper.

First and foremost, however, Barranquilla is famed for its carnival, held 40 days before Easter (end of February/beginning of March). It's reputed to be second only to Rio de Janeiro in terms of size and far less commercialized. In 2003 UNESCO declared it a "masterpiece of the oral and intangible heritage of humanity".

The city is surrounded by a continuous ring road, which is called the 'Vía Cuarenta' from the north along the river to the centre; 'Avenida Boyacá' to the bridge (Puente Pumarejo) across the Río Magdalena for Santa Marta; and 'Circunvalación' round the south and west of the city. The long bridge over the Río Magdalena gives fine views.

The central square is Plaza San Nicolás. Here is the former cathedral of **San Nicolás** and a small statue of Columbus. The commercial and shopping districts are around Paseo Bolívar (Calle 34), the main boulevard, a few blocks north of the old cathedral, and west along Avenida Murillo (Calle 45). A cultural centre, **Parque Cultural del Caribe**, has opened at the Paseo Bolívar end of Avenida Olaya Herrera (Carrera 46). It contains the **Museo del Caribe** ① *C 36, No 46-66, T5-372 0581, www. culturacaribe.org, Tue-Thu, 0800-1700, Fri 0800-1800, Sat-Sun 0900-1800, ticket office closes 1600 (1700 weekends), US$3.75,* an excellent introduction to the region. Displays are in Spanish only, but guided tours in English are available. Visits start on the top floor, at the Sala García Márquez, which has audiovisual displays and a library. Work your way down through floors dedicated to nature, indigenous people and cultures, to a video musical presentation at the end. Outside is a

1 Barranquilla centre

→ Barranquilla maps
1 Barranquilla centre, page 67
2 Barranquilla – El Prado, page 68

Where to stay
Cayenas 1
Girasol 2
San Francisco 3

Restaurants
La Cueva 1

Bars & clubs
Guararé 2

200 metres
200 yards

large open space for theatre and children's games, and the **Cocina del Museo** restaurant. Not far away is the restored customs house, **Antiguo Edificio de la Aduana** ⓘ *Vía 40 y C 36*, dating from 1919, which has historical archives.

West of the centre, opposite Parque La Paz, is the **Catedral Metropolitana** ⓘ *Cra 45, No 53-120*, which contains an impressive statue of Christ by the Colombian sculptor Arena Betancourt. To the northwest, the **Museo Romántico** ⓘ *Cra 54, No 59-199, Mon-Fri 0900-1200, 1430-1800, US$2.50*, covers the city's history with an interesting section on carnival. Visitors can also see some of García Márquez's old typewriters.

Stretching back into the northwestern heights overlooking the city are the modern suburbs of **El Prado**, Altos del Prado, Golf and Ciudad Jardín. There are good parks in these areas, including **Parque Tomás Suri Salcedo** on Calle 72.

Barranquilla also attracts visitors because the most important national and international football matches are held here in Colombia's largest stadium, **Estadio Metropolitano** ⓘ *Av Murillo, south of the city*. The atmosphere is considered the best in the country. Tickets can be bought from the official club store at shopping centre Portal del Prado in the city centre, or at the ticket windows of the stadium three hours before the match.

2 Barranquilla – El Prado

➡ **Barranquilla maps**
1 Barranquilla centre, page 67
2 Barranquilla – El Prado, page 68

Where to stay 🛏
Barranquilla Plaza 1
El Prado 2
Majestic 3
Meeting Point Hostel 4
Sonesta 5

Restaurants 🍴
Arabe Gourmet 1
Arabe International 2
Firenze Pizza 3
La Parrilla Libanesa 4
Los Helechos de Carlos 5

Bars & clubs 🍸
Flogg Club 6
Henry's Café 7

Beaches

Regular buses from Paseo Bolívar and the church at Calle 33/Carrera 41 travel 19 km to the attractive bathing resort of **Puerto Colombia** ① *www.puertocolombia-atlantico.gov.co*, with its pier built around 1900. This was formerly the ocean port of Barranquilla, connected by a railway. The beach is clean and sandy, though the water is a bit muddy. The **Hotel Pradomar** ① *C 2, No 22-61, T5-309 6011, www.hotelpradomar.com*, has a good beach bar, **Climandario Sunset Lounge**, and restaurant. It also offers surfing lessons, as does surf school **Olas Puerto Colombia** ① *T321-401 1526, www.olascolombia.com*. February to May is the best time for taking classes; the biggest waves are November to January. Nearby are the beaches of **Salgar**, and north of Barranquilla is **Las Flores** (2 km from the mouth of the Río Magdalena at Bocas de Ceniza); both are good places for seafood.

Along the Río Magdalena

South along the west bank of the Magdalena, 5 km from the city, is the old colonial town of **Soledad**. The cathedral and the old narrow streets around it are worth seeing. A further 25 km south is **Santo Tomás**, known for its Good Friday street theatre and processions in which flagellants symbolically whip themselves as an Easter penance. The small town of **Palmar de Varela** is a little further along the same road, which continues on to Calamar.

Parque Nacional Natural Isla de Salamanca ① *T312-577 7111, www.parqueislade salamanca.org, open 0830-1600, US$12 for non-nationals, US$4.55 for Colombians*, is a national park, across the Río Magdalena from the city, comprising the Magdalena Delta and a narrow area of beaches, mangroves and woods that separates the Ciénaga Grande de Santa Marta (see page 82) from the Caribbean. Its purpose is to restore the mangroves and other habitats lost when the highway to Santa Marta was built, blocking off the channels that connect the fresh and salt water systems. There is lots of wildlife, and there is an interpretation centre and guided walking trails (US$6-7.55) and canoe trips with guides (US$45-126 for groups of 10).

Listings Barranquilla *maps p67 and p68*

Tourist information

La Casa de Carnaval
Cra 54, No 49B-39, T5-319 7616, www.carnavaldebarranquilla.org.
The official carnival office and best place for carnival information.

Secretaría de Cultura
Patrimonio y Turismo, C 34, No 43-31, p 4, T5-339 9450, www.barranquilla. gov.co/cultura.

The main tourist office. Information is also available at the main hotels.

Tourist police
Plaza de San Nicolás.
Open 0800-1200, 1500-1700.

Where to stay

Hotel prices rise significantly during carnival; it's essential to book well in advance. Most people stay in the north zone, beyond the Catedral

Metropolitano, C 50. There are also a few hotels in the business zone, Cra 43-45, C 42-45.

$$$ Barranquilla Plaza
Cra 51B, No 79-246, T5-361 0333, www.hbp.com.co.
This deluxe hotel, popular with Colombian businessmen, it worth visiting just for the 360° view of the city from its 26th-floor restaurant. It has all the other amenities you would expect of a hotel of this standard, including gym, spa, sauna and Wi-Fi.

$$$ El Prado
Cra 54, No 70-10, T5-330 1530/40, www.hotelelpradosa.com.
A landmark in Barranquilla, this enormous hotel with 200 rooms has been around since 1930 and still retains some of its old-fashioned service. Fantastic pool shaded by palm trees, various restaurants, tennis courts and a gym.

$$$ Majestic
Cra 53, No 54-41, T5-349 1010, www. hotelmajesticbarranquilla.com.
An oasis of calm in the city, with large, fresh rooms. It has a fine pool and a restaurant serving the usual fish and meat dishes and sandwiches.

$$$ Sonesta
C 106, No 50-11, T5-385 6060, www.sonesta.com.
Overlooking the Caribbean, a 1st-class business hotel with fitness facilities and restaurant to match. There is a shopping centre and nightclub nearby.

$$ Girasol
C 44, No 44-103, T5-379 3191.
Safe, central with a helpful manager, it has a restaurant and a functions room.

$$ San Francisco
C 43, No 43-128, T5-351 5532, www.sfcol.com/barranquilla.html.
Bright rooms, courtyard full of songbirds, a good, safe bet, with restaurant.

$ Cayenas
C 43, No 44-136, T5-370 6912, www.cayenashotel.com.
A simpler option, welcoming, rooms are cheaper with fan.

$ Meeting Point
Cra 61, No 68-100, El Prado, T5-318 2599, www.themeetingpoint.hostel.com.
Very helpful and congenial Italian/ Colombian-owned hostel – the best choice for budget travellers. Mixed dorms or women only, US$10-15, cheaper with fan and shared bath, also has private rooms. Eating places and cultural centres nearby. Warmly recommended.

Restaurants

In Barranquilla you'll find places to suit all tastes and budgets. Many upmarket restaurants can be found along Cras 52-54 from C 70 to 93. There are numerous good Middle Eastern restaurants, especially Lebanese, in Barranquilla, due to waves of immigration in the 20th century; also Chinese restaurants and pizzerias.

$$$-$$ Arabe Gourmet
Cra 49C, No 76-181, T5-360 5930/358 3805, http://arabegourmetrestaurante.co.
More formal and expensive than other Arabic restaurants. There are others in the same chain.

$$$-$$ La Cueva
Cra 43, No 59-03, T5-379 0342/340 9813, www.fundacionlacueva.org. Closed Sun.

This cultural centre was formerly a high-class brothel and a favourite haunt of Gabriel García Márquez and his literati friends during the 1950s. Its bohemian charm may have gone, but its bar/restaurant is recommended for a visit. Good typical food, live music and other events.

$$$-$$ La Parrilla Libanesa
Cra 61, No 68-02, near Meeting Point, T5-360 6664, http://parrillalibanesa. amawebs.com.
Well-regarded Lebanese place, colourful, indoor and terrace seating.

$$ Arabe Internacional
C 93, No 47-73, T5-378 4700.
Good Arab cuisine in an informal setting.

$$ Firenze Pizza
C 68, No 62-12, El Prado, near Meeting Point, T5-344 1067, www.firenzepizza. com.co. Open 1500-2300
Pizza to eat in or take away.

$$-$ Los Helechos de Carlos
Cra 52, No 70-70, T5-345 1739, http:// restauranteshowloshelechos.com. Daily from 1000 (closes 1700 on Sun).
Offers *comida antioqueña* in a good atmosphere.

Bars and clubs

Carrera 8 is a popular nightlife area, but you'll need to take a taxi there and back.

Frogg Club
C 93, No 43-122, T5-304 8973, www.frogg.co.
Popular bar, good atmosphere.

Guararé
Cra 8 at C 35. T300-503 3303, Facebook: GuararéSalsaDisco. Open until 0400.
A good spot for salsa dancing.

Henry's Café
C 80, No 53-18, CC Washington, T5-345 6431. http://henryscafe.co. Daily from 1600.
Popular US-style bar and restaurant.

Entertainment

Teatro Amira de la Rosa, *Cra 54, No 52-258, T5-371 6690 ext 5153, www. banrepcultural.org/amira-de-la-rosa.* This modern theatre offers a full range of stage presentations, concerts, ballets, art exhibitions and more throughout the year.

Festivals

Jan/Mar Carnaval. Carnaval is a long-standing tradition in Barranquilla and is comparable to the carnivals in Rio de Janeiro and Trinidad. Pre-carnival parades and dances throughout Jan until an edict that everyone must party is read out. Carnaval itself lasts from Sat, with the Batalla de las Flores, through the Gran Parada on Sun, to the funeral of Joselito Carnaval on Tue. The same families have been participating for generations, keeping the traditions of the costumes and dances intact. Prepare for 4 days of intense revelry and dancing with very friendly and enthusiastic crowds, spectacular floats, processions, parades and beauty queens. Tickets for the spectator stands are sold in major restaurants and bars. As always on such occasions, take special care of your valuables. For more information, contact **La Casa de Carnaval**, www. carnavaldebarranquilla.org.

Shopping

There is a good-value handicrafts market near the old stadium, which is at Cra 46 y C 74 (at the end of Transmetro). **Portal del Prado**, www.portaldelprado.com, is one of the larger and more popular shopping complexes in the city.

Transport

Air Ernesto Cortissoz Airport, www. aerocivil.gov.co, is 10 km from the city. The airport has an ATM outside the terminal entrance, a *casa de cambio* in the hall (closed after 1900) and a tourist information desk. A city bus from the airport to town costs US$0.75 (more on Sun). Only take buses marked 'centro'; you can catch them 200 m from the airport on the right. Taxis are booked at the central taxi kiosk; tell them your destination and you will be given a ticket with the price to pay the driver at end of ride. A taxi to the centre costs US$10 and takes about 30 mins. From town, the bus to the airport (marked Malambo) leaves from Cra 44, travels up C 32 to Cra 38, then along C 30 to the airport.

There are daily flights to **Bogotá**, **Cali** and **Medellín**. International flights go to **Miami, Curaçao** and **Panama City**. Airlines include;

Avianca, C 53, No 46-38, T5-351 8344, and Cra 56, No75-155, local 102, T5-353 4989, at airport T5-334 8396; **Copa**, C 72, No 54-49, loc 1 y 2; **LAN**, C 75 No 52-56 local 3; **EasyFly**, T5-385 0676, www.easyfly.com.co; and **Viva Colombia**, T5-319 7989.

Bus Local Within the city, the **Transmetro**, www.transmetro.gov.co, is a dedicated bus service with 2 routes: *Troncal Murillo* and *Troncal Olaya Herrera*. It takes prepaid cards; single journey US$0.75 (a little more on Sun and holidays). Taxis for trips within town should cost US$2-4.

Long distance The main long-distance bus terminal, Km 1.5 Prolongación Murillo, www.ttbaq.com.co, is south of the city near the Circunvalación.

To **Santa Marta** with **Brasilia**, US$4.50, 2 hrs. To **Valledupar**, Copetran, 5-6 hrs, US$12. To **Bogotá**, 24 hrs, frequent, US$48-54, direct. To **Maicao**, US$1-18.25, 6 hrs (with **Brasilia** and others, frequent). To **Cartagena**, 2½-3 hrs, US$4.55, several companies. **Brasilia Van Tours** (Cra 35, No 44-63, T5-371 5226, as well as at the bus terminal) and **Berlinastur** (Cra 43, No 74-133, T318-396 9696, and other offices) have minibus services to **Cartagena** and **Santa Marta** (US$7).

Santa Marta
& around

Santa Marta, the capital of Magdalena Department, was the first town created in Colombia by the conquistadors. It does not have the same concentration of colonial beauty as Cartagena, but what it lacks in architecture, it makes up for in character and activity. The Samarios are some of the most welcoming and gregarious people you will find anywhere in Colombia.

The area around Santa Marta has much to offer, including a number of attractive beaches. To the west is the family resort of Rodadero; to the north is the former fishing village of Taganga. Backpackers love Taganga's lazy charm; it's a convenient stopping point en route to Tayrona and a good place to organize treks to Ciudad Perdida in the Sierra Nevada de Santa Marta. Southeast is Ciénaga de Santa Marta, 4000 sq km of wetlands with all types of waterbirds.

When leaving Santa Marta, most travellers will make a beeline for Tayrona National Park and its wild coastline of golden sands, secluded coves and tropical jungle. But there are other options. If the heat of the coast becomes too much, the rural village of Minca, in the foothills of the Sierra Nevada, will provide welcome respite. From Santa Marta you can also reach Aracataca, birthplace of Colombia's most famous writer, Gabriel García Márquez.

Essential Santa Marta and around

Getting around

Local bus services cost US$0.75 (this is a flat fee all the way to the airport and Rodadero); a taxi to Rodadero is US$5. Many of the buses coming from Barranquilla and Cartagena stop at Rodadero on their way to Santa Marta.

There are also local minibuses to Taganga US$1) and Tayrona. Boats from Santa Marta, Rodadero and Taganga visit beaches along the coast.

Tip...

The north end of town near the port and the section beyond the old railway station are dangerous and travellers are advised not to go there alone, as it's rife with drugs, and prostitution is common. South of Rodadero Beach has also been reported unsafe.

When to go

Santa Marta is always hot, although it can be marginally cooler in August and September. The driest months are December to April. October is the low season for tourists and also the wettest month.

Time required

You will need at least four days to see Santa Marta and Parque Nacional Tayrona; extend this to a week to trek to Ciudad Perdida.

Santa Marta

this lively city is a gateway to stunning beaches and mountains

Santa Marta lies at the mouth of the Río Manzanares, one of the many rivers that drain the Sierra Nevada de Santa Marta, on a deep bay with high shelving cliffs at each end. The city's fine promenade, Avenida R de Bastidas, offers good views of the bay and is lined with restaurants, accommodation and nightlife. At the southern end, where the main traffic turns inland on Calle 22, is a striking sculpture dedicated to the indigenous heritage of the region, La Herencia Tairona. The main commercial area and banks are mainly on Carrera 5, which has many kerbside stalls, and Calle 15, which leads to Plaza Bolívar. Carrera 3 is the hub of nightlife in the centre and is largely pedestrianized, as is Calle 19.

City centre

In the city centre, well-preserved colonial buildings and early churches still remain and more are currently being restored. The focal point is the pleasant and leafy Plaza Bolívar, which leads down to the seafront. It is complete with statues of Bolívar and Santander, as well as a bandstand. On the north side is the **Casa de la Aduana/Museo de Oro** ① C 14, No 2-07, which became the Custom House when Santa Marta was declared a free port in 1776. Previously it belonged to the church and was used as the residence of the Chief Justice of the Inquisition. The house dates from 1531 and was probably the first built of brick and stone in Colombia. An upstairs garret, added in 1730, offers an excellent view of the city and the bay. Simón Bolívar stayed here briefly in December 1830 and lay in state on the second floor from 17-20 December, before being moved to the cathedral. The Custom House now displays an excellent archaeological collection, with four rooms of exhibits mainly dedicated to the indigenous Tayrona. Especially interesting is the model

Santa Marta

Where to stay 🛏
1 Aluna Casa y Café
4 Casa Vieja
5 Hospedería Casa Familiar

6 La Brisa Loca &
   Agave Azul Bar
7 La Casa del Farol
8 La Casa Verde
9 Miramar
10 Nueva Granada
11 The Dreamer

Restaurants 🍴
1 Caribbean Wings
2 Donde Chucho
3 Donde L'Italiano
4 El Bistró
5 La Paila Caliente
6 Lulo
7 Merkabar

8 Ouzo
9 Ricky's

Bars & clubs 🎵
10 Oh La La, La Puerta

BACKGROUND

Santa Marta

This part of the South American coastline was visited in the early years of the 16th century by Spanish settlers from Venezuela. At this time, many indigenous groups were living on and near the coast, trading with each other and with communities further inland. The dominant group were the Tayrona.

Santa Marta was founded in 1525 by Rodrigo de Bastidas, who chose it for its sheltered harbour and its proximity to the Río Magdalena and therefore its access to the hinterland. The *indígenas* represented a potential labour force, and the gold in their ornaments suggested fortunes could be made in the area. Within a few years, the Spanish settlement was consolidated and permanent buildings, such as the Casa de la Aduana, had been constructed. Things did not go well, however. The *indígenas* did not 'cooperate', and there was continual friction amongst the Spaniards, all of whom were expecting instant riches. Bastidas' successor, Rodrigo Alvarez Palomino, attempted to subdue the *indígenas* by force, with great loss of life and little success. The *indígenas* that survived took to the hills, where their successors, the Kogi, remain to this day.

By the middle of the 16th century, a new threat had appeared. Encouraged, and often financed by Spain's enemies (England, France and Holland), pirates realized that rich pickings were to be had, not only from shipping, but also by attacking coastal settlements. The first raid took place around 1544, captained by the French pirate Robert Waal with three ships and 1000 men. He was followed by many privateers – the brothers Côte, Drake and Hawkins – who all ransacked the city. Forts were built on a small island at the entrance to the bay and on the mainland, but before the end of the century more than 20 attacks had been recorded; the pillage continued until as late as 1779, and the townsfolk lived in constant fear. Caches of treasure have been unearthed in old walls and floors around Santa Marta – testimony to the population's fear of looting during those troubled times. Cartagena, meanwhile, had become the main base for the conquistadors and much had been invested in its defences (see box, page 32). Santa Marta was never fortified in the same way and declined in importance.

Two important names connect Santa Marta with the history of Colombia. Gonzalo Jiménez de Quesada began the expedition here that led him up the Río Magdalena and into the highlands to found Santa Fe de Bogotá in 1538; and it was here that Simón Bolívar, his dream of Gran Colombia shattered, came to die. Almost penniless, he was given hospitality at the *quinta* of San Pedro Alejandrino, see below, where he died on 17 December 1830, at the age of 47.

of Ciudad Perdida, the most important of the Tayrona cities. Contained within the building is the **Museo de Oro (Gold Museum)** ① *T5-421 0251, http://proyectos. banrepcultural.org/museo-del-oro-tairona, Tue-Sat 0900-1700, Sun 1000-1500*, which holds a number of pre-Columbian gold artefacts in its vault.

The original building on the site of the **cathedral** ⓘ *Cra 4, C 16/17, Mass Mon-Fri 1200 and 1800, Sun 0700, 1000, 1200 and 1800,* was completed a few years after the founding of the city and was probably the first church in Colombia, as proclaimed by the inscription on the west front. The present building is mainly 17th century with many additions and modifications, hence the mixture of styles. There are interesting shrines along the aisles, a fine barrel roof and chandeliers, and a grey Italian marble altar decorated in red and brown. Look out for monument to Rodrigo de Bastidas, founder of the city, to the left of the main entrance, and the inscription by the altar steps commemorating the period when Bolívar's remains rested here from his death in 1830 to 1842 when they were transferred to the Pantheon in Caracas.

The **Convento de Santo Domingo** ⓘ *Cra 2, No 16-44, Mon-Fri 0800-1800, Sat 0800-1300,* now serves as the Centro Cultural Universidad Magdalena and houses a library as well as the **Museo Etnográfico de la Universidad del Magdalena,** which has good displays tracing the history of Santa Marta, its port and the Tayrona culture.

Quinta de San Pedro Alejandrino
5 km southeast of the city, T5-433 1021, www.museobolivariano.org.co. Daily 0900-1630 (1730 in high season). US$6, US$4.25 Colombians, discounts for children. To get there, take a bus or colectivo from the waterfront, Cra 1 C, towards Mamatoca and ask for the Quinta, US$0.75.

This early 17th-century villa on a sugar plantation is where Simón Bolívar lived out his last days; the simple room in which he died, with a few of his personal belongings, can be visited. Other paintings and memorabilia of the period are on display in the villa, and there's a contemporary art gallery featuring works by artists from Venezuela to Bolivia (the countries associated with Bolívar's life) and an exhibition hall in the grounds. The estate and gardens, with some ancient cedars, *samanes,* dignified formal statues and monuments, are worth a stroll. It is an impressive memorial to the man most revered by Colombians.

Listings Santa Marta *map p75*

Tourist information

Tourist office
On Plaza de la Catedral, C 16, No 4-15, T5-438 2587, www.santamarta.gov.co.
The main tourist office.

National parks office
C 17, No 4-06, Plaza de la Catedral, T5-423 0752, www.parquesnacionales.gov.co.
Has information for each of the 4 local parks.

Where to stay

Do not stay at the north end of town near the port and beyond the old railway station. It's essential to book ahead during high season, particularly weekends, when some hotels increase their prices by 50%.

$$$ La Casa del Farol
C 18, No 3-115, T5-423 1572, www.lacasadelfarol.com.

A luxury boutique hotel with 6 rooms, each with its own style, all modern conveniences, laundry service, beauty salon with massages and roof terrace with pool. Price includes breakfast.

$$$ La Casa Verde
C 18, No 4-70, T5-431 4122, www. casaverdesantamarta.com.
Only 5 suites, 'boutique' style, safe, small jacuzzi pool and juice bar. A *desayuno típico* is available.

$$ Aluna Casa y Cafe
C 21, No 5-72, T5-432 4916, www.alunahotel.com.
Pleasant and large Irish-run hostel in a converted 1920s villa, central and convenient. It has private rooms and dorms (US$7.55-9 pp), with roof terrace. Breakfast is extra. There's a café, extensive book exchange, and a good noticeboard. Recommended. Under same ownership is **Finca Entre Ríos**, www.fincaentrerios.com, 15 km from Santa Marta, a working farm with private and dorm rooms, full board $ pp

$$ Nueva Granada
C 12, No 3-17, T5-421 1337, www.hotelnuevagranada.com.
This charming old building in the historic quarter has rooms round a pleasant courtyard, quiet. Shared rooms with fan are cheaper ($). Safety deposit boxes in rooms, small pool with jacuzzi, includes breakfast and welcome drink. Reductions in low season. Recommended.

$$-$ Casa Vieja
C 12, No 1C-58, T5-431 1606, www.hotelcasavieja.com.
Has a Spanish feel about it with white tiling and simple, clean rooms and a/c. Cheaper with fan, welcoming.

$$-$ pp The Dreamer Hostel
Cra 51, No 26D-161 Diagonal, Los Trupillos, Mamatoco, T5-433 3264, or T300-251 6534, www.thedreamerhostel.com.
Travellers' hostel in a residential district 15 mins from the centre, on the way to Tayrona, 5 mins by taxi from the bus station. All rooms are set around a sunny garden and pool, dorms for 4-10 people and private rooms with and without bath, fan or a/c, bar, good Italian restaurant, tour information and activities, good atmosphere. All services close at hand, including a huge shopping mall, San Pedro Alejandrino and the bus stop for Tayrona. Recommended.

$ Hospedería Casa Familiar
C 10C, No 2-14, T5-421 1697, www.hospederiacasafamiliar.freeservers.com.
Run by an extremely helpful family, rooms with fan, roof terrace, and laundry service. Has information on diving and other activities, and organizes trips to Tayrona, Sierra Nevada and Ciudad Perdida.

$$-$ La Brisa Loca
C 14, No 3-58, T5-431 6121, www.labrisaloca.com.
US-owned lively hostel, with or a/c private rooms, all with shared bath. Meals extra. Also bar, swimming pool and billiard room.

$ Miramar
2 blocks from Malecón, C 10C, No 1C-59, T5-423 3276, www.hotelmiramar.com.co.
Very knowledgeable and helpful staff at this backpacker favourite. Can be crowded. Simple dorms and some nicer more expensive private rooms (US$15), motorbike parking, cheap restaurant. Often full. Reservations via the internet are held until 1500 on the day of arrival. Tours to the Ciudad Perdida, Tayrona,

Restaurants

$$$-$$ El Bistró
C 19, No 3-68, T5-421 8080. Daily 1100-2300, happy hour 1730-1930.
Meat dishes, pastas, salads, burgers, sandwiches and set lunches, not a large place and the menu is limited, wine list, Argentine influence throughout.

$$ Donde Chucho
C 19, No 2-17, T5-421 0861.
A little expensive but well situated in the corner of Parque Santander. Serves mostly seafood.

$$ Donde L'Italiano
Cra 3, No 16-26. Mon-Sat 1130-1430, 1800-2230.
Tasty Italian fare at reasonable prices, generous portions.

$$ La Paila Caliente
C 18, No 4-60, T5-421 4954.
Delightful restaurant with good Colombian/Caribbean food, à la carte at night, excellent value lunch.

$$ Ouzo
Cra 3, No 19-27, T5-423 0658, www.ouzosantamarta.com. Closed Sun.
Mediterranean, Italian, Greek restaurant and bar with seating on the street, popular.

$$ Ricky's
Cra 1a, No 17-05.
Beachside restaurant serving international food, including Chinese. Reasonably priced.

$$-$ Caribbean Wings
C 17, No 2-59.
Small *parilla* near the water with a sports-bar vibe. Popular for American-style chicken wings. Great option on a budget.

$$-$ Lulo
Cra 3, No 16-34, www.lulocafebar.com.
Café and bar serving *arepas*, wraps, paninis, fresh juices, coffee and cocktails.

$ Merkabar
C 10C, No 2-11. Opens early for breakfast.
Pastas, great pancakes, good juices and seafood. Family-run, good value and provides tourist information. Recommended.

Bars and clubs

Santa Marta is a party town; new clubs, discos and bars open every week. In the evening wander along Cra 3 and C 17 and 18 either side of it to see what's going on.

Agave Azul
C 14, No 3-74, Facebook: agaveazul.santamarta.
In the same building as **La Brisa Loca**. This Mexican bar is run by 2 brothers from San Francisco. It offers tasty food and good cocktails at affordable prices.

Oh La La Puerta
C 17, No 2-29.
Excellent bar and atmosphere in a colonial house. Recommended.

Festivals

Jul Festival Patronal de Santa Marta. Celebrates the founding of the city with parades and musical performances.
Jul Fiestas del Mar. Aquatic events and a beauty contest.

Guajira and local sites are available with the in-house operator. Airline tickets also sold here.

Shopping

Craft shops

The **market** is at C 11/Cra 11, just off Av del Ferrocarril and has stalls with excellent selections of hammocks. There are several good handicraft shops on Parque Bolívar. Also try **Artesanías Sisa** (Cra 4, No 16-42 on the Plaza Catedral, T5-421 4510), which sells local handicrafts including clothes, bags, hammocks and sombreros.

What to do

For trips to Ciudad Perdida and the Sierra Nevada, see under the relevant destination, below.

Tour operators

Aventure Colombia, *C 14, No 4-80, T5-430 5185, http://aventurecolombia.com.* Branch of the recommended Cartagena agency specializing in classic and alternative tours and expeditions across Colombia, focusing on trekking, eco and rural tourism.

New Frontiers Adventures, *C 27, No 1C-74, close to Playa Los Cocos, T318-736 1565/317-648 6786, www.colombia. newfrontiersadventures.com.* Trekking to Ciudad Perdida, birdwatching, diving and other adventures and ecotours, with English-speaking guides.

Turcol, *C 13, No 3-13, CC San Francisco Plaza loc 115, T5-421 2256, www. buritaca2000.com.* Arranges trips to Ciudad Perdida, Tayrona, Pueblito, Guajira and provides a guide service.

Transport

Air Simón Bolívar Airport is 20 km south of the city. A bus to town costs US$0.75; a taxi is US$12-50, less to Rodadero; beware of taxi drivers taking you to a hotel of their choice, not yours.

There are daily flights to **Bogotá**, **Bucaramanga**, **Cali** and **Medellín** for connections to other cities. During the tourist season, get to the airport early and book well ahead (the same goes for bus reservations). Airlines include **Avianca**, Cra 2A No 14-17, Edif de los Bancos, loc 105, T5-421 4958, T5-432 0106 at airport; **Copa**, CC Rex, Cra 3, No 17-27, loc 2; **EasyFly**, T5-435 1777; and **LAN**, C 23, No 6-18, loc 2.

Bus The **bus terminal** is southeast of the city, towards Rodadero. A minibus to the centre of Santa Marta costs US$0.75; taxi to the centre US$2.50, or US$5 to Rodadero.

Local To **Aracataca**, US$5 with **Berlinas**. Buses to **Taganga** can be picked up on Cra 5; buses to **Rodadero** leave from the waterfront. Buses to **Tayrona** leave from the corner of C 11/Cra 11 in the market area, every 15 mins, US$3.

Long distance To **Bogotá**, 7 daily, 16 hrs, US$35-52, **Brasilia** or **Berlinas del Fonce**. **Berlinas** and **Brasilia** to **Bucaramanga** about 9 hrs, US$25-28, frequent departures 0700-2200. Buses to **Barranquilla**, frequent, 2 hrs, US$4.50. To **Cartagena**, 5 hrs, US$13.50, with **Brasilia**. To **Riohacha**, 3 hrs, US$6.50-10. Frequent buses to **Maicao**, 4-5 hrs, US$15 a/c, cheaper non a/c. **Asotranstax** runs a door-to-door *colectivo* service to Mompós, which leaves Santa Marta 0300 and 1100, 6 hrs, US$40.

All along this stretch of coast are rocky headlands, sandy bays and coves, surrounded by hills, green meadows and shady trees. To the south, the bus from the airport passes by Playa Pleno Mar, one of the more tranquil and recommended beaches in the area. The best beaches east of Santa Marta are in Tayrona National Park, see page 85.

Around the bay
Santa Marta is the largest bay on this stretch of coast, with **Punta Betín**, a promontory, protecting the harbour to the north and a headland to the south on top of which are the ruins of an early defensive fort, **Castillo San Fernando**. There is a marine ecosystem research centre, run by Colombian and German universities, near the end of Punta Betín. If you wish to visit, you will need a boat or a permit to pass through the port area, so ask for guidance. The rugged **Isla El Morro** lies 3 km off Santa Marta and is topped by a lighthouse. The proximity of the port and the city means the beaches on the bay are not recommended for bathing.

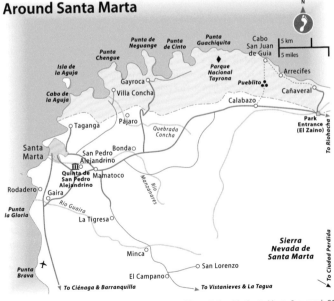

Around Santa Marta

N

5 km
5 miles

Punta de Neguange
Punta de Cinto
Punta Guachiquita
Cabo San Juan de Guia

Punta Chengue

Isla de la Aguja

Parque Nacional Tayrona

Pueblito

Arrecifes

Gayroca
Villa Concha

Cañaveral

Cabo de la Aguja

Calabazo

Taganga

Pájaro

Quebrada Concha

Park Entrance (El Zaino)

To Riohacha

Santa Marta

Bonda

San Pedro Alejandrino

Quinta de San Pedro Alejandrino
Mamatoco

Río Manzanares

Rodadero

Gaira

Río Guaira

Punta la Gloria

La Tigresa

Sierra Nevada de Santa Marta

To Ciudad Perdida

Minca

San Lorenzo

Punta Brava

El Campano

To Vistanieves & La Tagua

To Ciénaga & Barranquilla

Rodadero and around

Rodadero Beach, 4 km southwest of Santa Marta, is one of the best along this coast and is a popular destination for family holidays. It is part of the municipality of **Gaira**, a small town 2 km inland on the Río Gaira, which flows into the Caribbean at the southern end of Rodadero Beach. The main part of the beach has high-rise hotels of all standards, but it is attractive, tree lined, relatively clean and pleasant for bathing. Behind the promenade are restaurants, cheaper accommodation and other services. Nearby are a number of holiday flats and other facilities.

Launches leave Rodadero Beach at the end of Calle 12 for the 10-minute trip to the **Acuario y Museo del Mar del Rodadero** ⓘ *Cra 1 No 7-69, T5-422 7222, www.acuariorodadero.com, daily 0920-1600, US$12 including boat transport,* north along the coast at Inca Inca Bay, where you'll find sharks, dolphins, seals and many colourful Caribbean fish. The aquarium is linked to a small museum housing relics from Spanish galleons sunk by pirates, and a collection of coral and seashells. From the aquarium, you can walk (10 minutes) to **Playa Blanca** and swim in less crowded conditions. There is also food available at this beach.

Ciénaga de Santa Marta

South of Rodadero the paved coast road between Santa Marta and Barranquilla passes salt pans and skirts the Ciénaga Grande de Santa Marta. The wildlife sanctuary, recognized by UNESCO and RAMSAR, is not open to visitors, but many water birds, plants and animals can be seen on and around the lake. The construction of the coast road blocked the egress from the lake to the sea and killed large areas of mangrove, but a National Environment Programme is working to reopen the channels and restore the area. There are two villages built on stilts in the lake, **Nueva Venecia** and **Buenavista**. Ask at the Santuario de Flora y Fauna Ciénaga Grande de Santa Marta desk in the national parks office in Santa Marta (T5-423 0752, see Tourist information, page 77) about guides and boatmen who take visitors to the lake from the community of Tasajera. On the east shore of the lagoon is **Ciénaga**, which is famous for *cumbia* music.

Taganga and around

From Santa Marta it takes 15-20 mins by minibus (US$0.80) or taxi (US$5-6).

Close to Santa Marta is the former fishing village and beach of Taganga, where most people now make a living from tourism. Set in a tranquil semi-circular bay surrounded by scorched hills dotted with cacti, Taganga attracts its fair share of backpackers and has become quite a party resort, especially at weekends. It is laidback and welcoming, but beaches to the east of Tayrona National Park are becoming more favoured as 'in' places on the backpacker circuit (see page 87). The swimming is good, especially on **Playa Grande**, 25 minutes' walk round the coast or US$3 by boat, but do not leave your belongings unattended. Boat trips along the coast for fishing, and to the many bays and beaches, are run by hotels and by a syndicate of boatmen along the beach. Taganga is a popular place for diving and several well-established dive shops offer good-value PADI courses.

There is a good book exchange. An ATM that takes all major credit cards is next to the police station, half a block up from **Poseidon Dive Center**.

Half an hour north of Taganga is **Isla de la Aguja**, a good fishing zone. **Playa Granate** is nearer and has excellent places to snorkel and dive around the coral reefs, although lately the reefs have been showing signs of bleaching.

Listings Coast around Santa Marta *map p81*

Tourist information

Rodadero

Fondo de Promoción Turística
C 10, No 3-10, Rodadero, T5-422 7548.
Can provide local information and advice on hotels.

Where to stay

Rodadero
There are numerous resort hotels and holiday apartments; ask at the tourist information for a complete list. Do not stay in the area south of Rodadero Beach.

Taganga

$$$-$$ Bahía Taganga
C 8, No 1B-35, T5-421 0653,
www.bahiataganga.com.
Up on a hill at the north end of the bay with an unmissable sign on the cliff face. It has commanding views over the village and is tastefully decorated with clean rooms. Breakfast is served on a lovely terrace, hospitable, a/c, more expensive in the new building.

$$ La Ballena Azul
Cra 1, No 18-01, T5-421 9009,
www.hotelballenaazul.com.
Attractive hotel with a French Riviera touch, decorated in cool blues and whites. Comfortable, spacious rooms with sea views, cheaper with fan. Also runs boat tours to secluded beaches,

horses for hire. Nice restaurant on the beach, crêperie, terrace bar.

$$-$ Hostal Moramar
2 blocks uphill from beach opposite football pitch, CCa 4, No-17B-83, T5-421 9098.
Bright, airy patio area, Wi-Fi, breakfast and laundry extra, attentive owners, welcoming.

$$-$ La Casa de Felipe
Cra 5A, No 19-13, 500 m from beach behind football pitch, T316-318 9158 (mob), T5-421 9101, www.lacasadefelipe.com.
Cosy traveller place run by knowledgeable French team of Jean-Phillipe and Sandra Gibelin. Good kitchen facilities, excellent restaurant, hospitable, relaxing hammock and expansive roof with terrace with sea views, studio apartments, dorms (US$8-10.50) and rooms. Good information on trips to Tayrona (maps provided), English spoken.

$$-$ Techos Azules
Sector Dunkarinca, Cabaña 1-100, T5-421 9141, www.techosazules.com.
Off the road leading into town, *cabañas* with good views over the bay, private rooms and dorm US$8 pp (low season prices), free coffee, laundry service.

$ Bayview
Cra 4, No 17B-57, T5-421 9560, www.hosteltrail.com/bayview.

With a technicolour façade, pleasant rooms, cheaper dorms (US$7 pp), kitchen, barbecue area, lounges with DVD player.

$ Casa Blanca
Cra 1, No 18-161, T5-421 9232, at the southern end of the beach, Facebook: Hospedaje-Casa-Blanca.
Characterful. Each room has its own balcony with hammock, also has dorms. The roof terrace is a fine place to pass the evening, drinking beer with fellow guests. Also has a tour desk.

$ pp Divanga B&B
C 12, No 4-07, T5-421 9092, also Republika Divanga, C 11, No 3-05, T5-421 9217, www.divanga.com.
French-owned hostel, private rooms with or without bath or dorms (US$11-13), includes great breakfast in the B&B, breakfast not included at Republika, but rooms are cheaper, comfortable, 5 mins' walk from beach, nice views, attentive service, lovely atmosphere, good pool (at B&B). Also has Diva Expe tour operator and dive shop. Recommended.

$ Pelikan Hostal
Cra 2, No 17-04, T5-421 9057, www. hosteltrail.com/hostalpelikan.
Rooms with fan for 2-7 people, apartments, kitchen, laundry service, restaurant.

Restaurants

Taganga
Fresh fish is available along the beach and good pancakes can be found at the crêperie at the **Hotel La Ballena Azul**.

$$ Babaganoush
Cra 1C 18-22, 3rd floor next to the Tayrona Dive Center.
Serves up international dishes. Great steaks and a generous half-off happy hour from 1700-2200.

$$ Bitácora
Cra 1, No17-13.
Seafood, pastas, burgers, steaks and salads, has a good reputation.

Bars and clubs

Taganga

Mirador
C 1, No 18A-107, T301-638 8500, see Facebook, Mirador-de-Taganga.
Rooftop bar and disco that strikes a nice balance between in- and outdoor fun. Also has a hostel.

Sensation
C 14, No 1-04, T300-668 9144, Facebook: SensationTaganga.
Dance club that's open till 0300 at weekends.

What to do

Rodadero
In addition to trips to the aquarium, evening and day-long boat tours are offered (US$15-25), as well as swimming with dolphins (US$75).

Taganga
Adventure tours
Elemento, *C 18. No 3-31, T5-421 0870.* Mountain biking, hiking and other tours in the Sierra Nevada, Minca and Tayrona. **Vergel Tours**, *T304-571 1425, www. vergeltours.com.* The Vergel family organizes a number of excursions from Taganga, including trips to Ciudad Perdida, scuba outings, snorkelling and cliff jumping.

Diving

There are several dive shops in Taganga.
Oceano Scuba, *Cra 2, No 17-46, T5-421 9004, www.oceanoscuba.com.co.*
PADI, NAUI, TDI and other courses, 2, 3 and 4 days.

Poseidon Dive Center, *C 18, No 1-69, T5-421 9224, www.poseidondivecenter.com.* PADI courses at all levels and the only place on the Colombian Caribbean coast to offer an instructor course. German owner, several European languages spoken. Own pool for beginners. Wi-Fi.

Parque Nacional Natural Tayrona

increasingly touristy tropical idyll

Tayrona National Park is named after the Tayrona (also spelt Tairona) culture, one of the most important in pre-colonial Colombia. It extends from north of Taganga along 85 km of rugged coastline much of it fringed with coral reefs. The beaches are what you would expect of a tropical paradise: thick jungle teeming with wildlife spills over onto golden sand. You will see monkeys, iguanas and, possibly, snakes. Some beaches have pounding surf, while others are small, secluded bays, excellent for swimming and sunbathing.

Essential Parque Nacional Natural Tayrona

Finding your feet

The park has three entrances: Palangana for day visits to Neguanje, Gayraca and Playa Cristal; Calabazo for Pueblito and Cabo San Juan de Guía, and El Zaino, at the eastern end of the park, 35 km from Santa Marta, for Cañaveral and Arrecifes (El Zaino is the most commonly used).

The park is open daily 0800-1700; tickets cost US$12 for foreigners (regardless of age), US$4.55 for Colombians (US$2.45 children); parking is extra.

Tours can be arranged at several hotels and agencies in Santa Marta. Guides, who charge US$20 or more per person, are also available, but you will not need one for the main trail from Cañaveral to Arrecifes and beyond.

For further information see www. parquesnacionales.gov.co, or ask at the national parks office in Santa Marta (see page 77).

Getting around

In the wet, the paths are very slippery, so hiking boots are recommended.

From the gate *colectivos* make the 4-km journey to the visitor centre at Cañaveral (see below), US1.50, or it is possible to walk (approximately 30 minutes). You can hire horses to carry you and your luggage from Cañaveral to Arrecifes, US$8; La Piscina, US$13, or Cabo San Juan, US$16.50 (one way). It is possible to do a circuit Santa Marta–Cañaveral–Arrecifes– Pueblito–Calabazo–Santa Marta in one day, but you will need to leave by 0700 at the latest. It is easier (more downhill) to do the circuit in reverse, so ask to be dropped at Calabazo.

It is advisable to inform park guards when walking anywhere in the park other than the main trail.

There is something of the prehistoric about Tayrona. Half-close your eyes, and, with a little imagination, the flocks of pelicans that glide overhead could be pterodactyls; the bright-tailed lizards that scurry across the forest paths are reminders of their extinct cousins, and the enormous boulders that stand guard over the beaches look like they have been there since the beginning of time. However, time and tourism have caught up with Tayrona and it is becoming increasingly popular. Prices have rocketed and there is now a steady stream of visitors, especially during the national holidays of Semana Santa, July/August and December/January.

The western park

Many of the bays closest to Santa Marta are accessible by road, including the beautiful beach at **Villa Concha**, 5 km east of the city. Surrounded by tree-covered hills and with several restaurants nearby, the bay is popular with locals at the weekend and makes a good day trip during the week. Tours from Santa Marta visit this beach as well as **Neguanje** and **Playa Cristal** (a 10-minute boat ride from Neguanje). Neguanje can also be reached by *colectivos* from Santa Marta market, which leave at 0700 and return at 1600.

El Zaino and the eastern park

El Zaino, 35 km from Santa Marta, is the main access point for the eastern end of the park. From there, a road leads 4 km to the administrative and visitor centre at **Cañaveral**, where there is a gift shop, car park, a museum (closed at the time of writing), campsite, juice bar and a short trail to a viewpoint (about 30 minutes there and back).

It is a one-hour walk on a forest trail from Cañaveral to **Arrecifes**. The trail is mostly level, apart from a couple of short, steep sections; horses can be hired at Cañaveral for those that don't want to walk. At Arrecifes, beyond the cabins, campsites and eating places, is a long beach backed by mangroves. On no account be tempted to swim here as the tides and surf are treacherous. Every year, people drown because they do not heed the warnings.

Walk on from Arrecifes to **La Piscina**, 40 minutes further. You pass a little beach, **La Arenilla**, two-thirds of the way along, with a cevichería and juice stall. La Piscina also has a couple of places selling drinks and food. The beach is narrow, but the swimming after the walk is divine and there is excellent snorkelling. From La Piscina you can walk on to **Cabo San Juan de Guía**, 45 minutes, which also has excellent bathing, places to eat and a popular campsite/hammock place.

From Cabo San Juan you can return the way you came, take the boat to Taganga, or walk 1½ hours on a clear path up to the ruins of the ancient Tayrona settlement of **Pueblito**. A guided tour around the site is free, every Saturday, or as arranged with a park guard. There are still indigenous people at Pueblito; do not photograph them. From Pueblito you can continue for a pleasant two-hour walk up to Calabazo on the Santa Marta–Riohacha road. A circuit Santa Marta, Cañaveral, Arrecifes, Pueblito, Calabazo, Santa Marta in one day needs a 0700 start at the latest. It is easier to do the circuit in reverse, although the first two hours from Calabazo is uphill (start walking before 0700); ask to be dropped at Calabazo. Tours can be arranged at several hotels and agencies in Santa Marta.

It is advisable to inform park guards when walking in the park. Wear hiking boots and beware of bloodsucking insects. Take food, water and only necessary valuables. If you are staying overnight in one of the campsites or hammock places, remember to take all supplies with you as there is only a small store in the park.

East of Tayrona

Beyond El Zaino on the Santa Marta–Riohacha road is **Playa Los Angeles**, a fine empty stretch of coastline that's excellent for surfing. Ten minutes' walk west is the mouth of the Río Piedras, which forms the border of Tayrona National Park and is good for bathing. A short drive east of Tayrona, 5 km inland from Playa Costeño, is the **Quebrada de Valencia**, several natural swimming pools amid waterfalls, with good views. From the marked roadside entrance, it is a pleasant 20-minute walk along a clear path to the falls, with drinks and snacks available along the way. Note that the falls can get overcrowded during high season.

Listings Parque Nacional Natural Tayrona

Tourist information

The address of the national parks office in Santa Marta is given on page 77. Information can also be found at www.colombia.travel and www.parquesnacionales.gov.co.

Where to stay

Eastern park
Cañaveral and Arrecifes
Comfortable cabins ($) with thatched roofs (*Ecohabs*) for 1-4 people can be booked at Cañaveral, Arrecifes and other locations in or near the park, T311-600 1614, www.ecohabsantamarta.com. They offer privacy, great views over sea and jungle; they have decent restaurants.

Also at Arrecifes are various places to stay with double tents with mattress, US$5 pp (cheaper with own tent) and hammocks. These include **Bukaru**, T310-691 3626; Don Pedro, T322-550 3933; and **El Paraíso**, T317-676 1614.

Cabo de San Juan de Guía
There is a small restaurant with hammocks for hire (US$10-12.50) and 2 *cabañas* (US$60). Pitching your own tent costs US$10; double tent hire, US$25.

East of Tayrona
There is an ecohostel called **Yuluka** about 1 km from El Zaino entrance on the main road.

$$$ Cabañas Los Angeles
Los Angeles, T311-600 1614, www.cabanasantamartalosangeles.com.
Beachside apartments next to Tayrona National Park, with gorgeous sea views. Facilities include free breakfast, hammocks, large communal area and a restaurant. Choose from 4 different *cabañas*. The owner is Nohemi Ramos who also offers tours and hires out surfboards.

Restaurants

There are decent restaurants at both Cañaveral and Arrecifes, as well as smaller eateries at many of the beaches.

The Sierra Nevada, covering a triangular area of 16,000 sq km, rises abruptly from the Caribbean to 5800-m snow-capped peaks in about 45 km, a gradient comparable with the south face of the Himalaya and unequalled along the world's coasts. Pico Colón is the highest point in the country. Here can be found the most spectacular scenery and most interesting of Colombia's indigenous communities. The area has been a known drugs-growing, processing and transporting region. For this reason, plus the presence of guerrilla and paramilitary groups, some local *indígenas* have been reluctant to welcome visitors. But the situation is improving and limited activities are now possible, such as the trek to Ciudad Perdida. It is also possible to enter the sierra from Valledupar with permission from community leaders.

Ciudad Perdida

Entry US$6.50, US$2.75 for Colombians, US$1.25 children. For the latest information check with national parks offices in Santa Marta and Bogotá and the Fundación Pro Sierra Nevada, C 17, No 3-83, Santa Marta, T5-431 0551, www.prosierra.org.

Ciudad Perdida (Lost City) is the third of the triumvirate of 'must-sees' on Colombia's Caribbean coast (the other two being Cartagena and Tayrona). The six-day trek is right up there with the Inca Trail in Peru and Roraima in Venezuela, as one of the classic South American adventures and is a truly memorable experience.

Ciudad Perdida was called Teyuna by the Tayrona, meaning 'mother nature', and served as their political and trading centre. It was built around AD 700 at 1100 m on the steep slopes of Cerro Corea, which lies in the northern part of the Sierra Nevada de Santa Marta. The site covers 400 ha and consists of a complex system of paved footpaths and flights of steps linking a series of terraces and platforms on which were built cult centres, warehouses and residences housing between 1400 and 3000 people. Sophisticated irrigation systems and walls were constructed to prevent erosion. By around 1600 the Tayrona had been almost wiped out by the conquistadors and the few who survived were forced to flee. For the next four centuries, Teyuna disappeared under the forest growth. In 1973, tomb looters searching for gold, known to exist in burial urns and graves, rediscovered the city by chance. By 1975, the city was attracting local and international anthropologists and archaeologists who started to excavate, leading to the first tourist groups in 1984. Today the area is a protected indigenous reserve, where three main indigenous groups, the Kogis, Arhuacos and Arsarios (Wiwa), continue to live. For archaeological information, see **ICANH** ⓘ *C 12, No 2-41, Bogotá, T1-444 0544, www.icanh.gov.co.*

Trekking to the Ciudad Perdida The 20-km trek to the Lost City is perhaps as spectacular as the archaeological site itself. At times gruelling and challenging, it is not a leisurely walk, but is well worth the effort for a rewarding and

The Lost City

From the first day we set out on the trail toward the mysterious Colombian Lost City, until day six when the remarkable adventure into the heart of the sierra came to an end, I was blown away by the crystal-clear rivers that cascaded down from the upper reaches of the mountains and treated us to amazing natural swimming pools, beautiful waterfalls and a much welcomed respite after hours of hiking amidst the endless jungle landscape. There are 18 or so river crossings en route to the Lost City, river pools to swim in each day and 1200 stone steps to climb at the very end of the third day that take you above the gorgeous river valleys to the high ridges blanketed in green. While the site alone is impressive, and its mysterious history and late discovery only add to its splendour, the surrounding mountain peaks dominate the endless landscape. What else lies undiscovered and hidden among such wild, rugged and beautiful terrain?

Although there was a kidnapping incident on the trail in 2003, the region is currently considered safe and is heavily patrolled by the Colombian Army. The site is guarded day and night by about 40 friendly soldiers who pass their two-month assignment on site by asking visitors for cigarettes in exchange for odd looking nuts that they have picked up off the jungle floor. They will also obligingly pose for photos, which they seem to enjoy more than anything else.

There is more than one option when it comes to choosing a route, some a little more difficult and with longer days, but the rewards will outweigh the fatigue. Starting and finishing the hike in different places will give you the chance to see more of the remote landscape and travel to less visited parts of this unique mountain range.

Craig Weigand

memorable experience. Tours run all year, so be prepared for heavy rain. As well as lush tropical humid and dry forests rich in flora and fauna, there are crystal-clear rivers, waterfalls and natural swimming pools. Along the way, you will pass friendly Kogi villages. The final section involves climbing some 1200 steep, slippery steps to the summit of the city. Watch out for snakes.

All tours include: transport to and from the start and end of the trail at Machete Pelao (aka El Mamey), a settlement three hours east of Santa Marta; sleeping in hammocks with mosquito nets at organized camps or cabin sites; food; insurance; guides and entrance fees. The companies list the clothes and equipment you should take, such as sleeping bag, insect repellent, water bottle, etc. Don't forget that Ciudad Perdida is in a national park: it is strictly forbidden to damage trees and collect flowers or insects. Leave no rubbish behind and encourage the guides to ensure no one else does.

Minca

Catch a bus from C 11 between Cra 11 and 12 in Santa Marta (30 mins, US$2.50). A taxi will cost US$15-18.

If the heat of the coast becomes too much then a stay up in Minca is a refreshing alternative. Some 20 km from Santa Marta in the foothills of the Sierra Nevada, this small village, surrounded by coffee fincas and begonia plantations, is a popular excursion and offers several cheap and truly charming places to stay. Horse riding, birdwatching and tours further into the Sierra Nevada can be arranged from here.

About 45 minutes' walk beyond the village is **El Pozo Azul**, a local swimming spot under a waterfall. Popular at weekends but almost always empty during the week, it's well worth a visit. El Pozo Azul was a sacred indigenous site where purification rituals were performed and on occasion it is still used by the Kogi of the Sierra Nevada.

San Lorenzo

Beyond Minca, the partly paved road rises steeply to San Lorenzo which is surrounded by a forest of palm trees. On the way to San Lorenzo is **La Victoria**, a large coffee finca which offers tours to demonstrate the coffee-making process. It is possible to stay in *cabañas* run by the park authorities close by.

Near San Lorenzo is the **El Dorado Bird Reserve**, the perfect place to see the majority of the 19 bird species endemic to the Sierra Nevada de Santa Marta. It is managed by **ProAves** ① *Cra 20, No 36-61, Bogotá, T1-340 3229, www.proaves.org*, a Colombian NGO dedicated to the conservation of biodiversity, especially birds at risk of extinction. There is a lodge at the reserve and all visits must be arranged through ProAves. They run multi-day tours which include Minca and Guajira, or more specialist itineraries at set times.

Listings Parque Nacional Natural Sierra Nevada de Santa Marta

Tourist information

For the latest information, check with national parks offices in Santa Marta and Bogotá.

Fundación Pro Sierra Nevada (C 17, No 3-83, Santa Marta, T5-431 0551, www.prosierra.org) is also helpful.
For archaeological information, contact **ICANH**, C 12, No 2-41, Bogotá, T1-444 0544, www.icanh.gov.co.

Where to stay

Minca
There are many more places to stay in town.

$$$ Ecohabs Minca
T311-600 1614, www.ecohab santamarta.com.
Wood and thatch cabins for 2-8 people, with restaurant, bar, spa, activities and events organized, a good place for relaxation and birdwatching, transfers and packages can be arranged.

$$$ Minca-La Casona
On the hill to the right as you enter Minca,
T321-204 1965, www.hotelminca.com.
Converted convent with views of the
valley below, fully remodelled, with
breakfast, bath, fan, hot water, restaurant
and bar, various activities including
birdwatching.

$$ Sans Souci
Minca, T313-590 9213,
sanssouciminca@yahoo.com.
Rambling house in a beautiful garden,
German-owned, rooms in the house
or separate apartments, swimming
pool, kitchen, discount in exchange for
gardening. Stunning views.

$$ Sierra's Sound
C Principal, Minca, T311-600 1614,
www.mincahotelsierrasound.com.
Italian-owned, overlooking a rocky river,
hot water, home-made pasta, tours into
the Sierra Nevada.

What to do

Minca
Semilla Tours, *Minca, T313-872 2434,*
www.hosteltrail.com/tour_companies/
semillatours. Community tourism
company offering tours in the region
and elsewhere in Colombia. Also
volunteering opportunities.

Inland from Santa Marta
a detour for fans of Colombian literature and music

Aracataca
Aracataca, 60 km south of Ciénaga and 7 km before Fundación, is the birthplace
of Gabriel García Márquez. It was fictionalized as Macondo in some of his novels,
notably in *One Hundred Years of Solitude*. His home is now a **Casa Museo** ⓘ *take*
Cra 5 No 6-35 away from plaza at corner with Panadería Delipán, the museum is
next to La Hojarasca café, Tue-Sat 0800-1300, 1400-1700, Sun 0900-1400. Different
rooms have objects and quotations from his work in Spanish and English to
provide an overview of his family life. You can also visit the **Casa del Telegrafista**,
which houses a few dusty items. **Finca Macondo** (named after a type of tree) is
possibly the inspiration for García Márquez' choice of the name. You can visit it
in the afternoon, or take a tour in and around Macondo and to some outlying
towns, such as Sevilla. The tour takes five to six hours and can be arranged through
Primacho ⓘ *T321-593 7330, US$25* (see What to do, page 94). Other sites related
to the stories are the river, where you can swim, and the railway station, through
which coal trains pass.

Towards Valledupar
South of Aracataca and Fundación is the important road junction of Bosconia
(80 km). The main road continues to Bucaramanga, while a road west heads
towards the Río Magdalena; turn off this road at La Gloria to reach Mompós (see
Transport, below). The easterly route, meanwhile, heads towards Maicao and the
Venezuelan border reaching **Valledupar** after 89 km. Continuing on this road takes
you **Cuestecitas**, where you can turn north to Riohacha, or carry on to Maicao and
the Venezuelan border.

ON THE ROAD
Gabriel García Márquez

More than any other Colombian, Gabriel García Márquez, or Gabo as he is affectionately known, has shaped the outside world's understanding of Colombian culture. His books champion the genre of magical realism where the real and the fantastical blur so naturally that it is difficult to discern where one ends and the other begins.

But is this what life in Colombia is really like? Schoolteachers-turned-dictators who fashion a town's children into an oppressive army, a woman so beautiful she causes the death of anyone who courts her and a child born with his eyes open because he has been weeping in his mother's womb seem improbable, especially to sceptical Western sensibilities. Yet many of the places, events and characters are based on real life. Macondo, a place which features in so many of his stories, is modelled on his town of birth, Aracataca. Cartagena is easily recognizable as the unnamed port that is the setting for *Love in the Time of Cholera*, while Fermina Daza and Florentino Ariza's love affair is based on his own parents' marriage. Events in *Chronicle of a Death Foretold* and *The Story of a Shipwrecked Sailor* were inspired by real life stories lifted from newspaper articles.

Despite his death in April 2014, Márquez's legacy of combining fantasy and reality continues to be a defining characteristic of Colombia's artistic identity. And who can challenge Gabo's interpretation of the truth when Colombia has produced real life characters such as Pablo Escobar? Where else in the world are there villages that host donkey beauty contests or elect a mayor who dresses up as a superhero? Sometimes Colombian reality is stranger than Gabo's fiction.

Valledupar and around

Located on the plain between the Sierra Nevada de Santa Marta and the Sierra de Perijá, Valledupar is capital of César Department and the home of *vallenato* music and culture, now on UNESCO's Intangible Cultural Heritage list (see box, page 98). On the main Plaza Alfonso López Pumarejo is the cultural centre, **Compai Chipuco** ⓘ *C 16, No 6-05, T5-580 8710, tiendacompaichipuco@festivalvallenato.com*, which is a good place for information. It sells handicrafts, books and music and has a bar, restaurant and a photographic exhibition about Consuelo Araujonoguera, known as '*La Cacica*', one of the founders of Valledupar's famous music festival (El Festival de la Leyenda Vallenata, see page 94), who was murdered by FARC in 2001. Also of interest are **La Academia de Música Vallenata Andrés Turco Gil** ⓘ *C 31 No 4-265*, with photos of events and famous personalities, and **Casa Beto Murgas/Museo del Acordeón** ⓘ *Cra 17 No 9A-18, T300-836 8877, Mon-Fri 0900-1200, 1400-1700, Sat 0900-1200, US$4,* which has a collection of photographs, indigenous instruments and accordions.

Also on the Plaza Alfonso López Pumarejo is the **Iglesia Nuestra Señora de la Concepción** and the fine balconied colonial façade of the **Casa del Maestre**

Pavejeau, in front of which is a dramatic statue of 'La Revolución en Marcha' by Rodrigo Arenas Betancourt. Around the city are many other statues, some to symbols and instruments of *vallenato*. **Palenke Cultura Bar** (see Entertainment, page 94) offers dance classes. At the **Centro Artesanal Calle Grande** ① *C 16, block 7*, lots of stalls sell hats, bags, jewellery, hammocks and some musical instruments. (The **Exito** supermarket, Carreteras 6 y 7, Calle 16 y 17, has ATMs.)

The Río Guatapurí runs cold and clear from the Sierra Nevada past the city. The **Balneario Hurtado**, by the bridge just past the Parque de la Leyenda, is a popular bathing spot, especially at weekends, although the water is muddy after heavy rain. A statue of a mermaid overlooks the bathers from the trees, and there's food, drink and music on offer. To get there from the centre, take Carrera 9, the main commercial avenue; or, if cycling, the quieter Carrera 4. Across the bridge is **Ecoparque Los Besotes** (9 km), a dry forest wildlife reserve, good for birdwatching.

Casa Indígena ① *Av Simón Bolívar, just past the accordion statue at end of Cra 9*, is where the indigenous communities from the sierra gather. Go here if you need permission to visit remote places. A good excursion is to the Arhuaco community of **Nabusímake** ① *to get there take a bus at 0600 from Carrera 7A where it splits from Carrera 7 (beyond 5 esq) to Pueblo Bello (1½ hrs), then a jeep to Nabusímake (2-2½ hrs, US$5)*, one of the most important centres of indigenous culture in the Sierra Nevada de Santa Marta. You will have to stay the night as there is only one jeep each day and it comes straight back. Another full-day tour from the city is to **La Mina** (20 km), a natural swimming pool by magnificent rocks, also popular at weekends.

Listings Inland from Santa Marta

Where to stay

Aracataca

Most people visiting the town stay in neighbouring Fundación. **Restaurant El Patio Mágico de Gabo y Leo Matiz** occasionally organizes rooms.

$$-$ Hotel Milán
C 7 No 8-24.

Valledupar

$$$ Sonesta
Diag 10, No 6N-15, T5-574 8686, www.sonesta.com.
Business-class hotel, next to CC Guatapurí Plaza, it has all the usual amenities including a pool and restaurant.

$$ Casa de Los Santos Reyes
C 13, No 4A-90, T5-580 1782, www.hotelboutiquevalledupar.com.
Centrally located, this restored colonial home has been turned into a boutique hotel. Its 5 spacious rooms have all mod cons and there's a small pool. Run by the same people as **Hostal Provincia**.

$$ Hostal Provincia
C 16A, No 5-25, T5-580 0558, www.provinciavalledupar.com.
Private rooms and cheaper dorms for 6. A very good choice, with a nice atmosphere. Bike rental, Wi-Fi throughout, hammocks, barbecue and bar, lots of information, helpful staff can organize tours and excursions

to local indigenous communities.
Warmly recommended.

$$ Vajamar
Cra 7, No 16A-30, T5-573 2010,
www.hotelvajamar.com.
Smart city centre hotel with pool and
an expensive restaurant. Rooms are
cheaper at weekends.

$ Aqua Hostal
Cra 7 No 13A-42, T5-570 0439,
www.aquahostalvalledupar.com.
Hostel with private rooms as well as
12-bed dorms. Wi-Fi throughout.

Restaurants

Aracataca

$$ El Patio Mágico de Gabo y Leo Matiz
C 7 No 4-57.
Central option offers Italian and local
dishes in an open-air courtyard. Also has
vegetarian options.

$ La Hojarasca
Next to the Casa Museo. Daily 1800-2200.
Juices, snacks and drinks, clean
and pleasant.

Valledupar
There are some cafés on the Plaza
Alfonso López, but all types of
restaurants on Cra 9 from C 15 down,
heading towards Plaza del Acordeón.

$$ Varadero
C12 N0 6-56, T5-570 6175,
www.varadero.com.co.
Simply put: the best seafood in town.

$ Café de Las Madres
Pl de las Madres, Cra 9, No 15-19.
A nice shady place, with a limited
selection: coffee, beer, ices.

Entertainment

Valledupar
Palenke Cultura Bar, *Cra 5 No 13C 52.*
A good spot offering dance classes, free
cinema nights and other cultural events.

Festivals

Valledupar
6 Jan The anniversary of the founding
of Valledupar. There's dancing and
accordion music in the streets.
**Last week of Apr Festival de la
Leyenda Vallenata**. The festival
celebrating *vallenato* music and culture
draws thousands of visitors. It is focused
around Parque de la Leyenda. Contact
the cultural centre (C 16, No 6-05, T5-
580 8710, www.festivalvallenato.com)
for information.
Sep There are other cultural events
throughout Sep.

Shopping

Valledupar
Centro Artesanal Calle Grande,
C 16, block 7. Lots of stalls selling
handicrafts and local artwork,
including distinctive hats (US$15-
US$150), indigenous bags, jewellery,
hammocks and some musical instruments.
    Compai Chipuco, on the plaza. Sells
books and music CDs of the region.
    La Casa de la Música, Cra 9, No 18-85.
Books, music and CDs.

What to do

Aracataca
Primacho, *T321-593 7330.*
Arranges 5-hr tours of the town
and surroundings, US$25.

Valledupar

Paseo Vallenato Tour, *Diagonal 21, No 18-2 a 18-136, T313-571 9025, www. paseovallenato.com*. Offers cultural tours in and around Valledupar as well excursions to the river and indigenous communities. Recommended.

Transport

Aracataca

Bus To **Santa Marta**, US$3.35. To **Barranquilla**, US$5.25. To **Valledupar**, 3 hrs 45 mins, US$6 with **Cootracosta**. There may be a long stop in Fundación, but you don't have to change bus. To go to **Bucaramanga** (US$25) or **Bogotá** (US$35), you have to catch a bus coming from Santa Marta at the toll station (*peaje*) outside town 1½ hrs after the bus has left Santa Marta. Be at the toll 30 mins early. For information on all buses, go to the **Berlinas** office. Bicycle taxi from bus stop to centre US$0.65.

Valledupar

Air The airport is 3 km southeast of the town, close to the bus station (taxi, US$5).

Flights to **Barranquilla** (30 mins) and **Bogotá** (1½ hrs) with **Avianca** (T01-8000-953434) and **LAN** (Av Hurtado Diag 10N-6N, 15, CC Guatapuri, p 1, Plazoleta Juan Valdez). **Easyfly** (www.easyfly.com. co) also has flights from here.

Bus The bus terminal is near the airport (taxi, US$3.55).

To **Aracataca**, US$6.50. To **Santa Marta**, 4 hrs, US$7.55. To **Barranquilla**, 5-6 hrs, US$12.50. To **Cartagena**, US$15.75. To **Mompós** (via Bosconia) door-to-door service with local taxi/minibus driver Lalo Castro, T312-673 5226, US$20; if he isn't going, **CotraNorte**, **Cotracol** or **Cootracegua** buses leave every morning, or minibus from outside bus terminal to Santa Ana on the Río Magdalena, US$25, cross the Río Magdalena by bridge or take a ferry across to Talaigua Nueva, then motorbike taxi to Mompós, US$5-8. There are also door-to-door services to **Riohacha**, US$15, and **Bucaramanga**, 8 hrs, US$25-28.

Riohacha
& Guajira

Along the coast from Santa Marta the lush vegetation of the foothills of the Sierra Nevada gives way to flat expanses of scorched earth where only a scrub-like tree known as trupillo (*Prosopis juliflora*) and the cactus survive. The change in landscape marks the beginning of the Guajira Peninsula, home to the Wayúu, one of Colombia's best-preserved indigenous cultures. It is also the northernmost tip of South America and certainly feels like the end of the world: an arid and unforgiving terrain that is nonetheless home to vast flocks of flamingos and other birds.

Riohacha may be a departmental capital but it feels more like a sleepy fishing village, though it livens up considerably at the weekend and on public holidays. Musichi and Manaure, with their flamingos and salt works, will be of interest to nature lovers, and Cabo de la Vela, with its turquoise waters that lap against a desert landscape, is a sight to behold. If you have the time and energy, Parque Nacional Natural Macuira, an oasis of tropical green sprouting out of the semi-desert, and Punta Gallinas, the northernmost point of the continent, will cap off a trip into this strange and ethereal land. The difficulties in transport only add to the sense of adventure this peninsula presents.

Essential Riohacha and Guajira

Finding your feet

The Guajira Peninsula is bordered by the Gulf of Venezuela and the Caribbean Sea. Trips to the region are best arranged in Riohacha, but can also be organized in Bogotá, Cartagena and Santa Marta.

Getting around

Early morning is best for travel, as transport is scarce in the afternoon. Getting to Cabo de la Vela independently is a time-consuming and at times uncomfortable experience, particularly during the wet season, although it can be done: *colectivos* and taxis make the journey on the paved road to Uribia and Manaure, and from there on dirt tracks to Cabo de la Vela (two or three hours).

Beyond Cabo de la Vela we advise you take a tour or at least contract your own jeep and guide. **Aventure Colombia** in Cartagena (see page 47) arranges trips here from time to time.

When to go

Rainy season is September to November; dirt tracks can become impassable at this time. To enjoy the deserted beaches around Cabo de la Vela, avoid Christmas and Easter when it is crowded and full of cars. The **Festival of Wayúu Culture** in Uribia takes place in May.

Time required

Most tours of the peninsula last three days; add another couple of days' beach time to your itinerary.

Riohacha and around

fishing and flamingos

Riohacha, 160 km east of Santa Marta, is capital of La Guajira Department. Formerly a port, today it has the ambience of a provincial fishing town. *Riohacha y Los Indios Guajiros* by Henri Candelier, a Frenchman's account of a journey to the area 100 years ago, has very interesting depictions of the life of the Wayúu.

Palomino

The paved coastal road from Santa Marta crosses into Guajira Department at increasingly popular Palomino, halfway to Riohacha, which has a fine beach, a river running into the sea and views of the Sierra Nevada, including snow-capped Pico Bolívar. There are hotels, hostels and *cabañas* here, with more under construction.

Santuario Los Flamencos y Flora Los Flamencos
95 km east of Santa Marta and 25 km west of Riohacha, www.parquesnacionales. gov.co. Take a colectivo from the roundabout between the water tower and bus station in Riohacha to Camarones, US$3.

The Santuario de Fauna y Flora Los Flamencos covers 7000 ha of saline vegetation, including mangroves and lagoons, separated from the Caribbean by sand bars.

ON THE ROAD

Música tropical

No country in South America has a greater variety of musical genres than Colombia, and nowhere is music more abundant than in the fertile breeding grounds of the north coast. The diversity of musical expression comes from a mixture of African, indigenous and European influences.

On the coast, *música tropical* is an umbrella term used to encompass the many hybrids that have arisen over the years. Most popular among these is *vallenato*, a form of music that originated with farmers around Valledupar. Its primary instruments are the accordion; the *guacharaca* (a tube made from the trunk of a small palm tree, with ridges carved into it), which when scraped with a fork produces a beat, and the *caja vallenata* (a cylindrical drum brought over by African slaves).

Vallenato has its roots in a more ancient genre, *cumbia*, which is believed to derive from Guinean *cumbe* and began as a courtship dance practised among the slave population; it later mixed with European and indigenous instruments, such as the guitar, the accordion and the *gaita*, a type of flute used by the *indígenas* of the Sierra Nevada de Santa Marta. *Cumbia* is celebrated for bringing together Colombia's three main ethnic groups and was used as an expression of resistance during the campaign for Independence from the Spanish. *Cumbia* has many other derivatives, such as *porro, gaita, fandango* and *bullerengue*.

The newest genre to emerge is *champeta*. This is the most African of the genres; it takes its influence from *soukous* and *compas*, and is characterized by very sensual dancing. It gained popularity among the black population of Cartagena and San Basilio de Palenque in the 1980s.

The two large saline lagoons (Laguna Grande and Laguna de Navío Quebrado) are fed by several intermittent streams which form deltas at the southern point of the lakes and are noted for their colonies of flamingos. Some are there all year; others gather during the wetter months between November and May, when some fresh water enters the lagoons. The birds are believed to migrate to and from the Dutch Antilles, Venezuela and Florida. There is also plenty of other birdlife throughout the year.

Laguna Grande is near **Camarones**, which is just off the main road. From here another road leads to the park entrance at Guanebucane (3.5 km). At the northern end of **Laguna de Navío Quebrado** is a community-run visitor centre called **Los Mangles** ⓘ *T301-675 3862, www.ecoturismosantuario.weebly.com*, with *cabañas*, hammocks ($) and camping. Beware that it gets very windy and sleeping in hammocks can be uncomfortable. Meals are also available. The centre arranges birdwatching trips on foot or by boat (US$3 per person). Take plenty of water if walking. There are several bars/restaurants and two shops on the beach.

Riohacha

The city was founded in 1545 by Nicolás Federmann and became a centre for oysters; the pearls were valuable enough to tempt Drake to sack it. Pearling almost ceased during the 18th century and the town was all but abandoned. The town has two good white-sand beaches lined with coconut palms and divided by a long wooden pier. The sea is clean, despite the dark silt stirred up by the waves. A couple of blocks inland is the cathedral, where José Prudencio Padilla is buried. He was born in Riohacha and commanded the Republican fleet that defeated the Spaniards in the Battle of Lago Maracaibo in 1823. There is a statue of him in the central park that bears his name. Also worth visiting are the town's two busy markets: the old market in the centre and a newer one further south. At weekends Riohacha fills up, with bars and music springing up all over the place; it's a good

Riohacha

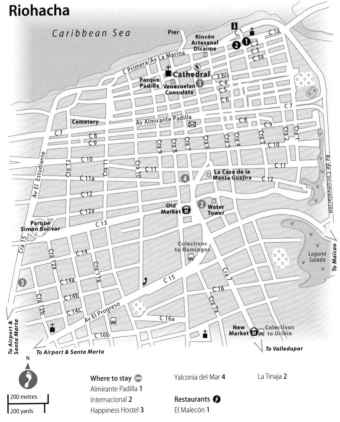

Where to stay
Almirante Padilla **1**
Internacional **2**
Happiness Hostel **3**

Yalconia del Mar **4**

Restaurants
El Malecón **1**

La Tinaja **2**

place to take stock before pushing on to Venezuela or into the more remote areas of La Guajira.

Maicao

The paved Caribbean coastal highway continues from Riohacha inland to Maicao, 78 km, close to the Venezuelan border. Maicao is hot, dusty and has a strong Arab presence, with several mosques and restaurants selling Arabic food. Clothing and white goods make up much of the business, but the city has a reputation for black-market activities. Most commercial premises close early and after dark the streets are unsafe. The border is 8 km east of Maicao at Paraguachón. With all the right papers, the crossing is easy.

Entering Venezuela There is no Venezuelan consul in Maicao, so if you need a visa, get it in Cartagena or Barranquilla (see page 131). Riohacha also has a consulate ① *Cra 7, No 3-08, p2, T5-727 4076, http://riohacha.consulado.gob.ve, Mon-Thu 0800-1200, Fri 0800-1300*, but it is not always easy to get a visa here, and you should check all requirements for your nationality before arriving. Note that a transit visa will only suffice if you have a confirmed onward ticket to a third country within three days.

Colectivos, known as *por puestos* in Venezuela, run from Maicao to Maracaibo, US$10 per person, or there is an infrequent microbus, US$3.50. There are very few buses to Venezuela after 1200. Brasilia bus company has its own security compound, where you can change money, buy bus tickets and food before your journey; non-passengers are not allowed in. *Por puestos* wait here for passengers to Maracaibo; it is a very easy transfer.

Entering Colombia If travelling by *por puesto* make sure the driver stops at the Colombian entry post. If not you will have to return later to complete formalities. Minibuses or *busetas* can be caught from the terminal de Maracaibo (T0261-723 9084) to Maicao for US$15, but they only run from 0400 to 0800. *Carritos*, taxis shared with three other passengers, continue to leave Maracaibo until 1500 (US$20 per person). **Migración Colombia** ① *C 5, No 4-48, Riohacha, daily 0800-1200, 1400-1700*.

Listings Riohacha and around *map p99*

Tourist information

The University of the Guajira has an excellent resource centre related to the region and the Wayúu culture (ID is necessary to get in). The provincial website is www.laguajira.gov.co and the municipal site is www.riohacha-laguajira.gov.co.

Dirección de Turismo de Guajira
C 1, Av de La Marina, No 4-42, T5-727 1015.
Offers some information, but you may find out more if you ask tour operators.

Where to stay

Palomino

$$ Finca Escondida
*Palomino, T310-456 3159, or 315-610
9561, www.chillandsurfcolombia.com.*
Double rooms, dorms at US$8-9 pp, also
camping and hammock space, direct
access to beach which has good surf,
surfing lessons, board rental, beach
sports, trekking or just lazing, bar-
restaurant, prices rise in high season.

$ pp The Dreamer on the Beach
*Playa Donaire, Palomino, T300-609 7229,
www.onthebeach.thedreamerhostel.com.*
Sister hostel to **The Dreamer** in Santa
Marta, dorms and private suites (**$$**),
gardens, pool, restaurant, mini-market
and access to activities.

Riohacha

$ Almirante Padilla
*Cra 6 No 3-29, T5-727 3612/2328,
hotel_almirante_padilla@yahoo.es.*
Crumbling but with character. Has an
inviting patio and a restaurant with
cheap *almuerzo*. It's clean, friendly, large
and very central. Some rooms with a/c.

$ Happiness Hostel
*Av Los Estudiantes, Cra 15, No 14-51,
T5-727 3828, http://happinesshostelcol.
wix.com/hostel.*
With private rooms (**$$**) and dorms with
bath (US$11.25 pp), bar, kitchen, patio,
can arrange tours.

$ Internacional
*Cra 7, No 13-37, T5-727 3483,
hriohachainternacional@gmail.com.*
A friendly option down an alleyway
off the old market, with a pleasant
restaurant on the patio. Free iced water.
Recommended.

$ Yalconia del Mar
*Cra 7, No 11-26, T5-727 3487,
hotelyalconiadelmar@hotmail.com.*
Rooms with bath, cheaper with fan,
clean, safe, friendly, helpful, halfway
between the beach and the bus station.

Maicao

$$$-$$ Hotel Maicao Internacional
*C 12, No 10-90, T5-726 8186,
hotelmaicao2009@telecom.com.co.*
Rooms with a/c, plus rooftop pool
and bar. A good option in Maicao,
attentive staff.

$$ Maicao Plaza
*C 10, No 10-28, T5-726 0310,
maicaoplazahotel@hotmail.com.*
Modern, central, with spacious rooms.

Restaurants

Riohacha

Many ice cream stalls, juice bars and
small *asados* serving large, cheap
selections of barbecued meat can be
found at the western end of the seafront.
There is also a row of picturesque,
brightly painted huts serving ceviche
and fresh seafood. The eastern end has
more restaurants for sit-down meals.

$$ El Malecón
C 1, No 3-47.
Good selection of seafood and meats
served in a palm-thatched barn looking
out to sea. There is music and dancing
in the evenings. A good place for
people-watching.

$$ La Tinaja
C 1, No 4-59.
Excellent seafood in a light, breezy
restaurant. Try the tasty and
substantial *delicias de la casa* rice dish.
Recommended.

Hammocks

There's no better way to enjoy Colombia's beaches than to relax in a hammock, using conveniently located palm trees as supports. Plenty of places hire them out, but for true comfort it's best to buy your own.

The hammocks developed by the Wayúu are made up of intricately woven threads of cotton that form a crocheted net. These are known as *chinchorros* and are larger than the average hammock, with wrap-around sides that serve as a blanket and elaborate tassels. The best places to buy chinchorros are the market in Riohacha and Uribia's handicraft shops in La Guajira.

The other most common style uses brightly coloured woven cotton or wool to form a large stretch of material. These can be bought in San Jacinto, a couple of hours south of Cartagena, which is the capital of Colombia's hammock industry and the best place to find a bargain. The market in Santa Marta also has a good selection.

Festivals

Riohacha
Mar Festival Francisco el Hombre. *Vallenato* festival, www. festivalfranciscoelhombre.com.

Shopping

Riohacha
Good hammocks sold in the new market, 2 km from town on the road to Valledupar. The best place for buying local items is **La Casa de la Manta Guajira** (Cra 6 y C 12). Be prepared to bargain.

What to do

Riohacha
Tour operators
Trips to the Guajira Peninsula are best arranged in Riohacha where there are several operators. Tours to Cabo de la Vela, 1-2 days, usually include Manaure (salt mines), Uribia, Pilón de Azucar and El Faro. Afternoon tours to Wayúu *rancherías* include a typical goat lunch.

Cabo de la Vela Turismo, *T5-728 3684, www.cabodelavela.turismo.co.* Runs tours throughout the region.
Comfaguajira, *T5-727 0204, www. comfaguajira.com. Mon-Fri 0800-1200, 1400-1700.*
Kaí Ecotravel, *Diagonal 1B, No 8-68, Uribia T5-717 7173, or 311-436 2830, also at Hotel Castillo del Mar, C 9A, No 15-352 in Riohacha and in Hotel Juyasirain, Uribia, www.kaiecotravel.com.* Based in Uribia and run by a network of Wayúu families, this operator organizes 2-day tours to Cabo de la Vela (US$127 pp), 4-5-day tours to Parque Natural Nacional Macuira (US$505 pp) and 3-day tours to Punta Gallinas (US$330 pp) and up to US$825 for an 8-day full circuit. Prices are per person for 2 people and include transport, accommodation and food; discounts for larger groups.

Transport

Riohacha
Air The **José Prudencio Padilla Airport** is south of the town towards Tomarrazón.

There are daily flights a day to **Bogotá**, 1 hr 35 mins, with **Avianca** (C 7, No 7-04, T727 3914), for connections to other cities.

Bus The main bus terminal is on C 15 (Av El Progreso)/Cra 11. Some *colectivos* for Uribia and the northeast leave from the new market, 2 km southeast on the Valledupar road. It is best to travel from Riohacha in a luxury bus, in the early morning, as these are less likely to be stopped and searched for contraband.

Brasilia runs Pullman buses to **Maicao**, frequent service, 1-1½ hrs, US$6.50; also to **Santa Marta**, US$6.50-10, 3 hrs, and **Cartagena**, US$18, every 30 mins. There are no direct buses to **Cabo de la Vela**; travel to **Uribia** and wait for a jeep (see below).

Taxi Coopcaribe Taxis travel throughout the region and can be picked up almost anywhere in town, especially close to the old market area near the **Hotel Internacional** or outside **Drogas La Rebaja**. They charge US$10 to either **Uribia** (1½ hrs) or **Manaure** (1¾ hrs) and leave when full (4 people); be prepared to pay slightly more if there are no other travellers.

Maicao
Bus There is a bus terminal to the east of town with frequent services to **Riohacha**, US$5; **Santa Marta**, 3 hrs, US$13; **Barranquilla**, 4-5 hrs, US$17-18.25, and **Cartagena**, 6 hrs, US$24. Those who decide against taking a flight to Venezuela via Panama can opt for a taxi or bus from Riohacha to Maicao and then a *colectivo* to Maracaibo (see page 100).

Guajira Peninsula
beautiful and remote indigenous outpost

Beyond Riohacha to the east is the arid and sparsely inhabited Guajira Peninsula, with its magnificent sunsets. The indigenous peoples here, the Wayúu, fish, tend goats and collect *divi-divi* pods from a strangely wind-bent tree (the *Caesalpina coriaria*), which are mainly used for tanning. (Look out for the coloured robes worn by the women.) This is a semi self-governing zone, but increasingly, thanks to government schemes, the Wayúu are also involved in tourism. The local language is Wayuunaiki; beyond Cabo de Vela little Spanish is spoken.

Manaure and Musichi
Manaure ① *www.manaure-laguajira.gov.co*, is known for its salt flats southwest of the town. Hundreds of workers dig the salt and collect it in wheelbarrows: a bizarre sight against the glaring white background. If you walk along the beach for an hour, past the salt works, there are several lagoons where flamingos gather. Around 14 km from Manaure in this direction is **Musichi**, with a protected area for the flamingos, **Area Natural Protegida de los Flamencos Rosados**. Note that the birds may be on the other side of the lagoon and difficult to see, so take binoculars. To get there, hire a moto-taxi or rent a bicycle in Manaure. Take plenty of sunblock and water, and remember a torch for returning in the evening.

Uribia

Uribia is known as the indigenous capital of Colombia, but it doesn't really live up to its name. You can buy authentic local handicrafts by asking around, but it's also full of Venezuelan contraband and has a rough and ready feel to it. There is a **Wayúu Festival** here annually in June at which *alijunas* (white people) are welcome, but ask permission before taking photographs.

Cabo de la Vela
From Uribia busetas run until 1400, few on Sunday, US$6-10; all transport leaves from the market.

The journey from Uribia to Cabo de la Vela via Puerto Bolívar is uncomfortable and slow, as passengers are dropped off at their various *rancherías*, but it is also spectacular; the final few kilometres are a bumpy ride across a shimmering, dried-out salt lake that generates mirages. Cabo de la Vela, known as 'Jepirra' in Wayuunaiki, is where the Wayúu believe their souls go after death. The barren landscape of shrubs and cacti only serves to accentuate the colour of the water, which glimmers in a dozen shades of aquamarine. At night, don't forget to look up for spectacular starry skies. In recent years tourism has really taken off here, and there are now more hostels in Cabo de la Vela than in Riohacha itself, all of them following the two-mile bay. There are excursions from Cabo de la Vela to Pilón de Azúcar mountain, which has lovely views of the sea, and to a beautiful beach and lighthouse.

Parque Nacional Natural Macuira
For information, C 8, No 5-73, T5-728 2636 in Riohacha. Mon-Fri 0800-1200, 1400-1600, entry US$11.25, Colombians US$3.75, children US$2.40, registration and 30-min compulsory induction at Nazareth park office, open Mon-Fri 0700-1200, 1400-1700, guides US$20.

Towards the northeast tip of the Guajira Peninsula is the **Serranía de Macuira**, named after the Makui people, ancestors of the Wayúu. The 25,000-ha park is entirely within the Wayúu reservation and consists of a range of hills over 500 m, with microclimates of their own creating an oasis of tropical forest in the semi-desert. The highest point is **Cerro Palúa**, 865 m, and there are two other peaks over 750 m. Moisture comes mainly from the northeast, which forms clouds in the evening that disperse in the early morning. The average temperature is 29°C and there is 450 mm of mist/rain annually providing water for the streams that disappear into the sand once they reach the plains.

Macuira's remoteness has resulted in some interesting flora and fauna; notable wildlife includes the cardinal bird and 15 species of snake, including coral snakes. There are also Wayúu settlements little affected by outsiders, where the indigenous people cultivate cashew nuts, coconuts and plantains, as well as collecting *divi-divi* pods. The rangers are all locals and are very friendly.

To reach the Parque Nacional Natural Macuira you must travel northeast from Uribia along the mineral railway, then either round the coast past Bahía Portete, or direct across the semi-desert, to Nazareth on the east side of the park. There are no tourist facilities anywhere nearby and no public transport, though trucks may take you from Bahía Portete to **Nazareth** (seven to eight hours in the dry season), if you can find one. Nazareth is a Wayúu village and the location of the park office where you must register, pay and undergo an induction before entering the park. Someone may let you stay the night in a hammock here; otherwise, there is camping beside the park office.

Spending a few days exploring the park is a remarkable and rewarding experience. The landscape, usually arid

Tip...
The Guajira Peninsula is not a place to travel alone; you are strongly advised to join a tour group, but if travelling independently, then parties of three or more are recommended. Always check the situation before setting out. The roads are mostly dirt tracks and can be in very bad condition or even impassable during the wet season. Also remember it is hot; it is easy to get lost; there is limited mobile phone reception and very little water.

and desolate, turns a bright shade of green after the rainy season and there are gorgeous bays for swimming and chilling. It's also the best place for getting closer to Wayúu culture and traditions. A recommended walk is a visit to the 40-m-high **El Chorro waterfall**, a delightful lush, green area. At the tip of the park, spectacular **Punta Gallinas** is the northernmost point in South America. When the road is bad, it can only be reached by a two- to three-hour boat ride from near Cabo de la Vela, often choppy and very wet. Nearby is **Taroa**, where sand dunes drop directly into the sea. It's a dramatic spot for a swim, but beware of the powerful waves and strong currents.

Listings Guajira Peninsula

Where to stay

Manaure and Musichi

$$ Palaaima
Cr 6, No 7-25, T5-717 8455/314-581 6789, irisfaep@hotmail.com.
Comfortable, cool rooms with a/c or fan. There are always Wayúu locals hanging around the hotel who are eager to talk about their culture and traditions.

Uribia
There are other cheap, somewhat grotty options.

$ Hotel Juyasirain
Diagonal 2A No 2B-02, T5-717 7284, juyasirain2009@hotmail.com.
The only slightly more upmarket hotel in Uribia. Large, light and airy with a patio restaurant.

Cabo de la Vela
This area becomes very crowded during high season, but there are 60 hostels to choose from, mostly basic with hammocks, but some have TV and a/c. There is a telecom centre. Most places have hammock space on the

beach, US$5-10. Fish meals cost US$4-6, including a large breakfast.

Parque Nacional Natural Macuira

$ Luz Mila
Punta Gallinas.
A lonely but friendly little hostel and restaurant run by the Wayúu, where **Kaí Ecotravel** (see below) has a base for their tours. Recommended.

What to do

Uribia
Kaí Eco Travel, *Diagonal 1B, No 8-68, T5-717 7173, or T311-436 2830, also at Hotel Castillo del Mar, C 9A, No 15-352, in Riohacha and in Hotel Juyasirain, www.kaiecotravel.com.* Run by a network of Wayúu families. Organizes tours to Cabo de la Vela (for 2 days, US$127 pp for 2 people, discounts for larger groups), Parque Natural Nacional Macuira (for 5 days US$505 pp for 2 people), Punta Gallinas (for 3 days US$330 pp for 2 people), up to US$825 for a 8-day full circuit, including transport, accommodation and food. Highly recommended.
Kaishi, *T5-717 7306/311-429 6315, www.kaishitravel.com.* Speak to Andrés Delgado. Jeep tours around La Guajira.

Transport

Manaure and Musichi
Early morning *busetas* to **Uribia**, 30 mins, US$3.

Uribia
All transport leaves from the market. *Busetas* to **Maicao**, 1 hr. Also *busetas* to **Puerto Bolívar**, daily until 1400 (fewer on Sun), for onward transport to **Cabo de la Vela** (US$6-10 for the whole journey). The journey is slow as passengers are dropped off at their various *rancherías*.

San Andrés
& Providencia

San Andrés and Providencia are islands that most Colombians dream about visiting at least once in their lifetime. Closer to Nicaragua than to the Colombian mainland – there is a running dispute between the two countries over sovereignty – these Caribbean islands have what locals have dubbed 'the sea of seven colours', though it often seems like more. At 32 km in length, the Old McBean Lagoon barrier reef off Providencia is the third largest in the world. The waters around this archipelago play host to a variety of marine life, and the clarity of the sea makes this one of the best diving destinations in the Caribbean. In 2000, the Archipelago of San Andrés, Old Providence and Santa Catalina was declared a UNESCO World Natural Heritage Site called the Seaflower Biosphere Reserve.

San Andrés and Providencia share a coastline rich in coral reefs, white-sand cays and waters of extraordinary colours, but are in fact very different. San Andrés, the larger island, is a popular mass tourism destination, replete with resort hotels and discos. Providencia has quietly observed its big sister's development, decided it does not want to follow the same path, and has put in place certain restrictions to halt the encroachment of package tourism.

Essential San Andrés and Providencia

Finding your feet

The islands are 770 km north of continental Colombia, 849 km southwest of Jamaica and 240 km east of Nicaragua. A cheap way to visit San Andrés is on a package from Bogotá or another major city, with flights, accommodation and food included; look for supplements in the Colombian newspapers and adverts on the internet. Alternatively, you may wish to opt for a cheap airfare and choose where to stay when you get there. On arrival in San Andrés, you must buy a tourist card, US$22.50; it is also valid for Providencia, so don't lose it. You must also have an onward or return ticket. Visitors to Providencia can arrive by air from San Andrés (20 minutes) or by sea on launches and boats that ferry goods over. Beware that the sea can be choppy on this trip.

Getting around

Cars, motorbikes, bicycles and golf buggies can all be hired on San Andrés, but they may be in poor condition. Buses ply the route along the east coast and there are taxis, too. On Providencia, transport is provided by *chivas* and *colectivos* or by hiring a moped or golf buggy. Boats go to offshore cays.

When to visit

The islands have a typical Caribbean climate that includes hurricane season from roughly June to November. The best weather is from December to April, but these months also attract the largest crowds.

San Andrés is a coral island, 11 km long, rising at its highest to 104 m above sea level. The town, commercial centre, major hotel sector and airport are at the northern end of the island. A good view of the town can be seen from El Cliff. San Andrés is a popular, safe and local holiday destination for Colombians.

Sights

San Andrés and Providencia are famous in Colombia for their different styles of music: the local form of calypso, soca, reggae and church music, as well as schottische, quadrille, polka and mazurka, the musical legacies of the various European communities that settled here. A number of good local groups perform on the islands and in Colombia. Look out for concerts at the **Coliseo San Luis** on the east coast and the cultural centre in San Andrés town. There is also a **Museo Casa Isleña** ① *Ctra Circunvalar Km 5, daily 0900-1800, US$3.50*, housed in a small historic building with displays relating to the culture of the island, including food, music and dance.

The eastern side of the island has beautiful cays and beaches backed by hotels and resorts; perhaps the best is at **San Luis** and **Bahía Sonora** (Sound Bay). If you can tear yourself away from the sand, visit **Hoyo Soplador** at the southern tip of the island, a geyser-like hole through which the sea spouts into the air when the wind is in the right direction. The west coast is less spoilt, but there are no beaches on this side. Instead there is **El Cove**, the island's deepest anchorage, and **Cueva de Morgan** (Morgan's Cave), reputedly a hiding place for pirate's treasure, which is penetrated by the sea through an underwater passage. Next to Cueva de Morgan is a **Pirate Museum** ① *US$3*, with exhibitions telling the history of

1 **San Andrés Island**

Punta Norte
Johnny Cay
Bahía Sardinas
Punta Hansa
San Andrés
Punta Paraíso
Roca del Pescador
Bahía de San Andrés
Caribbean Sea
Baptist Church
Bahía Baja
Museo Casa Isleña
La Loma (120m)
El Acuario
La Laguna
Haynes Cay
Cueva de Morgan
Rocky Cay
San Luis
El Cove
Bahía Sonora
Monte Derecho
La Piscinita
Hoyo Soplador
Punta Sur

N

1 km
1 miles

Where to stay 🛏
Casa Harb **1**
Sunset **2**

Restaurants 🍴
Bibi's Place **1**

➡ **San Andrés maps**
1 San Andrés Island, page 109
2 San Andrés town, page 112

BACKGROUND
San Andrés and Providencia

Columbus spotted the islands on his fourth trip to the Caribbean in 1503. Their early colonial history was dominated by the conflicts between Spain and England, though the Dutch also occupied Providencia for some years. English Puritans arrived on Providencia from Bermuda and England in 1629 and later moved to San Andrés. The English left in 1641, but Creole English remained the dominant language until recent times and is still widely spoken. Surnames such as Whittaker, Hooker, Archbold, Robinson, Howard and Newell are also common. Providencia later became a pirate colony, shared between the Dutch and the English, before it was taken by the Spanish and assigned to the Vice Royalty of New Granada (modern-day Colombia) in 1803. In 1818 French Corsair Louis-Michel Aury successfully invaded Providencia and declared it part of the United States of Argentina and Chile, using it to capture Spanish cargo to bolster the burgeoning Latin American Independence movement. Finally, in 1822 San Andrés, Providencia and Santa Catalina were incorporated into the newly independent state of Gran Colombia.

The inhabitants of the islands are mostly the descendants of Jamaican slaves brought over by English pirates such as Henry Morgan, although the frequent comings and goings of English, Dutch, French and Spanish settlers over the years has led to an extraordinary genealogical mix. Today, about 50% of the population of San Andrés is made up of immigrants from mainland Colombia, and there are also Lebanese and Turkish communities. Immigration is less pronounced in Providencia. The islands' proximity to Nicaragua (just 240 km west) has led that country to claim them from Colombia in the past. Battleships now patrol San Andrés to guard against any invasion.

the coconut, lots of paraphernalia salvaged from wrecks around the island and a replica pirate ship. About 1 km south of Cueva de Morgan is **West View** ① *daily 0900-1830*, an excellent place to see marine life as the sea is very clear. There is a small jetty, with a diving board and slide, and a restaurant opposite the entrance.

From El Cove, you can cross the centre of the island back to town. Here you will find some life as it was before San Andrés became a tourist destination, with clapboard houses and traditional music. You'll also pass **La Laguna**, a freshwater lake 30 m deep, home to many birds and surrounded by palm and mango trees. Just to the north is **La Loma**, the highest point on the island at 104 m. On the town side of La Loma is the first **Baptist Church** to be built on the island (1847), which serves as a beacon to shipping. The church has a Sunday service 1000-1200 with gospel singing. If you take a turning just before the church you will reach the **Mirador Escalona**, a lookout point on someone's unfinished roof (US$1.50), from which there are spectacular views of the island.

Offshore cays

Boats leave from Tonino's Marina or from Muelle Casa de la Cultura on Avenida Newell in San Andrés between 0930 and 1100 daily for El Acuario and Haynes Cay, and continue to Johnny Cay (frequently spelt Jhonny) in the afternoon (US$10), returning at 1530. **El Acuario** has crystalline water and is a good place to snorkel and see eagle and manta rays. You can wade across the water to **Haynes Cay** where there is good food and a reggae bar at **Bibi's Place** ① *daily 0930-1530.* **Johnny Cay** has a white beach where parties are held every Sunday. These are popular tours; if you want to avoid the crowds a good option is to hire a private boat (US$150 for the day) and do the tour in reverse.

Other cays and islets in the archipelago are **Bolívar**, **Albuquerque**, **Algodón** (included in the Sunrise Park development in San Andrés), **Rocky**, the **Grunt**, **Serrana**, **Serranilla** and **Quitasueño**.

Diving

Diving off San Andrés is very good; the depth varies from three to 30 m, visibility from 30 to 60 m. There are three types of site: walls of seaweed and minor coral reefs; large groups of different types of coral, and underwater plateaux with much marine life. It is possible to dive in 70% of the insular platform. The **Pared Azul** (**Blue Wall**) is excellent for deep-water diving. **Black Coral Net** and **Morgan's Sponge** are other good sites.

Listings San Andrés *maps p109 and below*

Tourist information

Tourist office
Av Newball No 6-30, opposite Restaurante La Regatta, T8-512 5058, secturismosai@yahoo.com. Mon-Fri 0800-1200, 1400-1800. Staff are helpful and speak English. They can provide maps and hotel lists.

There's also a **tourist kiosk** at the end of Av 20 de Julio, across from the sea, daily 0800-2000. The municipal website is www.sanandres.gov.co and the island's newspaper, the *San Andrés Hoy*, www.sanandreshoy.com, has some information in Spanish.

Where to stay

Hotels quote rates per person, but we list prices for double rooms. Prices include half board, but most can be booked without meals. Most raise prices by 20-30% on 15 Dec. This also applies to Providencia. The Decameron group has 5 hotels on San Andrés, www.decameron.co.

$$$$ Casa Harb
C 11, No 10-83, T8-512 6348, www.casaharb.com.
Just outside town, this boutique hotel takes its inspiration from the Far East and is the most stylish location on the island. Each room is individually decorated with antique furniture. The baths, made of solid granite, are enormous. A former

family home, this mansion has an infinity pool and offers home-cooked meals.

$$$$ Lord Pierre
Av Colombia, No 1B-106, T8-512 7541, www.lordpierre.com.
It boasts a magnificent pier on the tip of the *malecón*, but some of the services are a bit dated. Rooms are large with heavy furniture.

$$$ Portobelo
Av Colombia, No 5A-69, T8-512 7008, www.portobelohotel.com.
Occupies a couple of buildings on western end of the *malecón*. Rooms have large beds, a/c and cable TV. Breakfast included. ($$$$ in high season).

$$$ Sunset Hotel
Ctra Circunvalar, Km 13, T8-513 0420, www.sunsethotelspa.com.
On the western side of the island, this is the perfect place to stay if you want to do some serious diving – or just want to escape the crowds. It has bright, fresh rooms with high ceilings, all set around a saltwater swimming pool. With a restaurant serving a mixture of international and regional food in a typical clapboard house and a dive shop next door, this is one of the best places to unwind in San Andrés.

$$$-$ pp El Viajero Hostel
Av 20 de Julio No 3A-122, T8-512 7497, www.elviajerohostels.com.
A member of the South American El Viajero hostel chain. It has private rooms and dorms (US$19 per bed) all with en suite bath, a/c and safe boxes. Breakfast included in the price, bicycles can be hired, rooftop bar and scuba certification courses. There's a tourist office at reception that books all tours and excursions. Like its sister hostel in Cartagena, El Viajero is for the party crowd.

$$ Hernando Henry
Av Las Américas, No 4-84, T8-512 3416, www.hotelhernandohenry.com.
At the back of town, this hotel has shoddy but passable rooms. TV and laundry service. Rooms are significantly cheaper with fan.

$$ La Posada D'Lulú
Av Antioquia, No 2-28, T8-512 2919/523 6308.

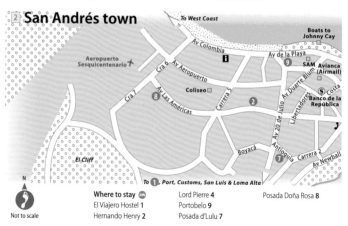

San Andrés town

To West Coast

Boats to Johnny Cay

Av Colombia

Av de la Playa

Aeropuerto Sesquicentenario ✈

Cra 6 Av Aeropuerto

SAM Avianca (Airmail)

Cra 7

Av Las Américas

Coliseo

Carrera 5

Costa

Banco de la República

Av 20 de Julio

Av Duarte Blum

Libertadores

Boyacá

Antioquia Carrera 2

Av Newball

EL Cliff

To Port, Customs, San Luis & Loma Alta

N

Not to scale

Where to stay
El Viajero Hostel 1
Hernando Henry 2

Lord Pierre 4
Portobelo 9
Posada d'Lulu 7

Posada Doña Rosa 8

This brightly coloured hostel with its clean and comfortable rooms is one of the best mid-range options in town. There are 2 apartments to rent for longer stays and an excellent restaurant serving home-cooked food. Recommended.

$$ Posada Doña Rosa
Av Las Américas con Aeropuerto, T8-512 3649, www.posadarosa.blogspot.com.
A 2-min walk from the airport, this is a reasonable and economical option. It has clean rooms with private bathrooms and a small patio with potted plants. There is a kitchen and TV room, and it's a short walk from the beach. Also has 2 apartments to rent.

Restaurants

$$$-$$ La Regatta
Av Newball, next to Club Náutico, T8-512 0437, www.restaurantelaregatta.com.
Seafood restaurant on a pier, fine reputation.

$$$-$$ Margherita e Carbonara
Av Colombia, No 1-93, opposite the Lord Pierre Hotel.

Italian-owned restaurant decorated. Good pizzas.

$$ Bibi's Place
Haynes Caye, www.bibisplace.com.
Reggae bar and restaurant on cay next to **El Acuario** serving seafood, including crab and lobster. Organizes full moon parties and civil and rasta weddings.

$$ Niko's
Av Colombia, No 1-93.
Bills itself as a seafood restaurant though its steaks are actually better. Lovely setting by the water.

Festivals

Jan Festival del Cangrejo. Celebrating the crab and all the many ways it can be prepared to eat, plus music and dancing.
20 Jul Independence, which incorporates a **Festival del Mar.**
Sep Green Moon Festival. A popular music festival that has been revived after several years' absence.
End-Nov Reinado del Coco. The crowning of the Coconut Queen coincides with the festival of the island's patron saint.
Dec Rainbow Festival. Reggae and calypso music.

What to do

Canopying
Canopy La Loma, *Vía La Loma-Barrack.*
A site at the top of the hill in San Andrés. 3 'flights' over the trees (450 m, 300 m and 200 m above sea level) with spectacular views out to sea. Good safety precautions and equipment.

Diving
Banda Dive Shop, *Hotel Lord Pierre, Local 104, T8-513 1080, www.bandadiveshop.com.*

➡ **San Andrés maps**
1 San Andrés Island, page 109
2 **San Andrés town, page 112**

Restaurants ❶
La Regatta **1**
Margherita e Carbonara **2**

Niko's **3**

PADI qualified, offers various courses. Fast boat and good equipment.

Sharky Dive Shop, *Ctra Circunvalar Km 13, T8-512 0651, www.sharkydiveshop. com*. Next to **Sunset Hotel**, Sharky's has good equipment and excellent, English-speaking guides. PADI qualifications and a beginners' course held in the Sunset's saltwater pool.

Water sports and boat trips

Cooperativa Lancheros, *on the beach in San Andrés town*. Fishing trips, windsurfing, jet skiing and kitesurfing. Snorkelling equipment can be hired for US$5.

Galeón Morgan, *Centro Comercial New Point Plaza, T8-512 8787*. Boat tours to El Acuario.

Air The airport is 15 mins' walk from town. Buses to the centre and San Luis go from across the road; a taxi is US$5.50-7.50, a *colectivo*, US$1.

It is essential to confirm flights to guarantee a seat. Schedules change frequently. To **Providencia,** twice daily with **Satena** (San Andrés, T8-512 1403; Providencia, T8-514 9257) and **Searca** (booked through Decameron, www.searca.com.co); bookable only

in San Andrés. Flights to **Bogotá**, **Cali**, **Medellín** and **Cartagena** with **Avianca** (Av Colón, Edif Onaissi local 107, T8-512 3212, airport T8-512 3216); **Satena** and **Searca**. **Copa** (Av Newball, No 4-141, Torre Sunrise Beach, local 125-B6) has a daily flight to **Panama City**.

Boat From **Providencia**, **Catamaran Sensation**, www. catamaransananandresyprovidencia. com, sails Mon, Wed, Thu, Fri, Sun 0800, returning at 1430, US$42 one way, 4 hrs. Alternatively, cargo boats make the journey 3 times a week, 4 uncomfortable hrs, US$65 (return); they usually leave at 0600-0700, arriving at 1130. *Miss Isabel*, *Doña Olga* and *Raziman* make the trip regularly; speak directly to the captain at the port on Bahía San Andrés.

Bus and taxi Buses run every 15 mins along the eastern side of the island, US$1, and more often at night and during the holidays. Taxis around the island cost US$15-20, but in town fares double after 2200.

Vehicle and bicycle hire Cars, motorbikes, bikes and golf buggies can all be hired, up to US$40 per day. A licence is required to hire cars and motorbikes, and a passport may be required as deposit.

Providencia, also called Old Providence, 80 km to the north-northeast of San Andrés, is 7 km long and 3.5 km wide. The island is more mountainous, rising to 360 m, and considerably more verdant than San Andrés due to its volcanic origin. There are waterfalls, and the land drops steeply into the sea in places.

Providencia is striving to retain its cultural identity: hotels must be constructed in the typical clapboard style of the island and cannot be built higher than two storeys; mainland operators cannot manage them directly, but must work in partnership with local owners; only locals are allowed to buy property on the island, and outsiders can stay no longer than six months at a time.

Providencia

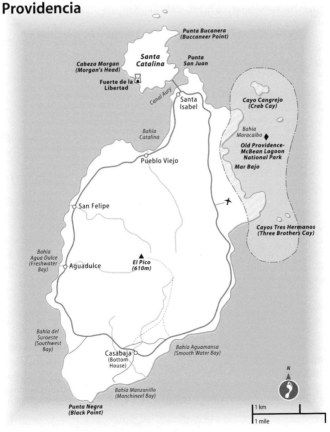

ON THE ROAD

The black crabs of Providencia

With the arrival of the first rains between April and June, Providencia is the scene of a spectacular natural phenomenon. Each night during the wet season thousands of black crabs (*Gecarcinus lateralis*) descend from the forests of High Hill and release their eggs in the waters between South West Bay and Freshwater, wriggling their abdomens in the surf to deposit their eggs. The hatchlings are born in the sea and return to the hills one month later.

During the migration the road that encircles the island is closed to traffic, thus allowing the crabs free access to the beaches without the risk of being run over. **Coralina** (www.coralina.gov.co), the government's environmental agency on the archipelago, has banned the capture and eating of crabs during the breeding season and anyone caught disobeying the ban risks a heavy fine equivalent to three months of the minimum wage.

Many of the islanders make a living from crab fishing, but during this time the hunters turn protectors, as they are employed as enforcers of the ban, thus ensuring that Providencia's black crab population will continue to thrive.

Parque Nacional Natural Old Providence – McBean Lagoon

In 1996 part of the east coast and offshore reefs and coral islands were declared a national park (entry US$4.50 for non-nationals). **Cayo Cangrejo** (Crab Cay) is a beautiful place for swimming and snorkelling; at the southern end of the national park is **Cayos Tres Hermanos** (Three Brothers Cays). Recommended diving spots on the Old McBean Lagoon reef are **Manta's Place**, a good place to see manta rays; **Felipe's Place** where there is a submerged figure of Christ; and **Stairway to Heaven**, which has a large wall of coral and big fish.

The land position includes **Iron Wood Hill** (150 m), whose tree species include cockspur (*Acacia colinsii*), which has large conical-shaped needles that are home to a species of ant (*Pseudo-myrmex ferruginea*) with a very painful sting.

In the south of the island, there are superb views from **Casabaja** (Bottom House) or **Aguamansa** (Smooth Water). From here, a climb to the summit of **El Pico** (360 m) will take about one hour and cost US$15 with a guide. You will see relics of the fortifications built on the island during its disputed ownership.

Santa Catalina

Boat trips can be made to Santa Catalina, an old pirate lair separated from Providencia by a channel cut for better defence. Santa Catalina is joined to the main island by a 100-m wooden bridge, known as the **Puente de los Amantes** (Lovers' Bridge). An ATM is tucked away just before the bridge, on the road to Santa Catalina. On the west side of Santa Catalina are the ruins of an old fort, built by the English to defend their pirate colony. Formerly known as Fort Warwick, it was rechristened **Fuerte de la Libertad** after the island was retaken by the Spanish in the 17th century. The fort still has the original canons and it is rumoured that there is a secret cave below that was used by Henry Morgan to escape to the sea (probably untrue). Beyond the fort is **Playa del Fuerte**, a fine beach, excellent for snorkelling, with caves with air chambers and lots of starfish. Further still is a rock formation called **Morgan's Head**; seen from the side it looks like a man's profile. The path beyond Morgan's Head leads through thick forest to the top of the mountain and an abandoned house formerly belonging to a drug trafficker.

Beaches
The largest, most attractive and least developed beach is **Bahía Manzanillo** (Manchineel Bay) at the southern end of the island, which is named after the *manzanillo* trees found on its edges. (The fruit is like a miniature apple; it is sweet-smelling but has an acid taste and is poisonous.) It has a couple of restaurants, including **Roland's Roots Bar**. A good walk over Manchineel Hill from Bottom House (Casa Baja) will take you 1.5 km through tropical forest, with fine views of the sea, to **Bahía del Suroeste** (South West Bay); many types of bird can be seen on the route, along with iguanas and blue lizards. South West Bay is fringed by almond trees, palms and has bottle-green water. On Saturday afternoons the local boys hold bareback horse races here. To the north, **Bahía Agua Dulce** (Freshwater Bay) has a small strip of beach and several sea-front hotels. Between Agua Dulce and San Felipe is **Alan's Bay**, which is very secluded and seldom visited.

Listings Providencia map p115

Tourist information

Tourist office
In the Centro Administrativo Aury,
T8-514 8054.

Where to stay

Rooms can be rented at affordable prices in local houses (*posadas nativas*). Hotels in Agua Dulce are 10 mins by motor taxi (US$1) from centre or 1-hr walk. Suroeste is a 20-min walk from Agua Dulce. The Decameron group, www.decameron.co, represents 5 properties on the island, including **Cabañas Miss Elma** (T8-514 8229, www.hotelmisselma.com) and **Cabañas Miss Mary** (T8-514 8454, www.hotelmissmary.com) at Aguadulce.

$$$$ Deep Blue Hotel
Maracaibo Bay, T8-514 8423/ 315-324
8443, www.hoteldeepblue.com.
Luxury 'boutique' hotel set in tropical forest. It offers splendid views of Crab Caye and the Caribbean. There's a restaurant by the sea and visitors get complimentary use of the hotel's sea kayaks. It has an infinity pool and staff can arrange scuba diving and other excursions. Good sustainability and environmental policies. Recommended.

$$$ Posada del Mar
Agua Dulce, T8-514 8168,
www.decameron.co.
Pink and purple clapboard house with comfortable rooms, each with a terrace and hammock looking onto the bay. The sea laps at the edge of the garden.

Has cable TV, a/c, minibar and hot water. Recommended.

$$$ Sol Caribe Providencia
Agua Dulce, www.solarhoteles.com.
Bright chain hotel offering 2- to 5-night packages, with pool, sea views, a/c, TV, fridge.

$$$-$$ Sirius
South West Bay, T8-514 8213, www.siriushotel.net.
Large, colourful house set back from the beach, run by a Swiss family. The rooms are large and light, some have balconies with hammocks. Kitchen available for guests. Also dive centre, kayaks, wakeboarding, horse riding, massage. The owner speaks German, Italian and English. Half-board and diving packages available.

$$ Hotel Old Providence
Diagonal Alcaldía Municipal, Santa Isabel, T8-514 8691, Facebook: Hotel-Old-Providence.
Above supermarket **Erika**, rooms are basic but clean and have a/c, cable TV, fridge and private bathroom.

Restaurants

Local specialities include crab soup and *rondón*, a mix of fish, conch, yucca and dumplings, cooked in coconut milk. Corn ice cream is also popular – it tastes a little like vanilla but sweeter. Breadfruit, a grapefruit-sized fruit with a taste similar to potato, is the archipelago's official fruit.

As well as hotel restaurants, good places include: **Arturo**, on Suroeste beach, next to Miss Mary, and **Café Studio**, between Agua Dulce and Suroeste, which serves great pies and spaghetti.

$$ Caribbean Place (Donde Martín)
Aguadulce.
Bogoteño chef Martín Quintero arrived for a brief stay in 1989 and has never left. He uses local ingredients. Specialities include lobster in crab sauce, fillet of fish in ginger, and corn ice cream.

$$ Roland's Roots bar
Playa Manzanillo, T8-514 8417, rolandsbeach@hotmail.com.
Parties at Roland's bar-restaurant are legendary. The menu is mainly seafood. He also hires out tents ($).

Shopping

Arts and Crafts Café, *Agua Dulce, T8-514 8297.* The French owners sell local crafts and delicious home-made cookies and ice cream.

What to do

Diving
Felipe Diving, *South West Bay, T8-851 8775, www.felipediving.com.* Mini and full courses, also rents snorkel equipment, can arrange lodging. Owner Felipe Cabeza even has a diving spot on the reef named after him. Warmly recommended. See also **Hotel Sirius**, above. PADI qualifications.

Snorkelling and boat trips
Snorkelling equipment can be hired from numerous outlets or on board. Day tours are arranged through hotels around the island, stopping typically at Cayo Cangrejo to swim and snorkel. Other recommended snorkelling sites include the waters around Santa Catalina, where there are many caves to explore as well as **Morgan's Head** and lots of starfish; **Hippie's Place** on the northwest coast, which has a little bit of everything; and **El Faro** (The Lighthouse), at the end of

the reef before it drops into deep sea, some 14 km from Providencia.

Tour operators

Body Contact, *Aguadulce, T8-514 8283.* Owner Jennifer Archbold organizes excursions, fishing and hiking trips, currency exchange, accommodation, and more. Recommended.

Chivas (brightly coloured buses) circle the island at more or less regular intervals; the standard fare is US$2. *Colectivos* can also be found on the island and charge much the same. Agua Dulce is 10 mins by motor taxi (US$1) from the centre or a 1-hr walk. Suroeste is a 20-min walk from Agua Dulce. Mopeds and golf buggies are available for hire (up to US$40 per day).

Practicalities

Getting there

Air

Most international fights arrive at Bogotá from where there are onward connections to Cartagena (see page 47 for airport information), Barranquilla and San Andrés with several of the airlines listed below. Fares are significantly cheaper outside the peaks times of Easter, July, August and December to mid-January.

From Europe

There are flights to Bogotá with **Avianca** from Barcelona and Madrid, **Iberia** from Madrid, **Air France** from Paris and **Lufthansa** from Frankfurt.

From North America

Avianca flies to Bogotá from several North American cities: New York, Miami, Orlando, Los Angeles, San Francisco and Washington. Other carriers from North America are **American** (Miami), **Delta** (Atlanta, New York), **United** (Houston, Newark), **Jet Blue** (Fort Lauderdale, Orlando), **Spirit** (Fort Lauderdale) and **Air Canada** (Toronto). International fights direct to Cartagena go from Fort Lauderdale (**Spirit**), Miami (**Avianca**) and New York (**Jet Blue**). There are also fights to Barranquilla from Miami (**Avianca**).

From Latin America

Bogotá can also be reached from many Latin American and Caribbean cities with **Avianca**, **LAN**, **Copa**, **Tame**, **Avianca Ecuador** (formerly **AeroGal**), **Conviasa** and **AeroMéxico**. There are direct flights to Cartagena and Barranquilla from Panama (**Copa**).

Road

To get to Cartagena from neighbouring countries overland, the only possibility is by road from Venezuela (see page 100). It is not possible to enter Colombia from Panama (see page 63) by road.

Sea

There are few options for arriving in Cartagena by sea. These are limited to cruise ships, tourist boats sailing between Panama and Cartagena (see page 48) and local pleasure trips.

Getting around

Air

Avianca ① *www.avianca.com*, is the national carrier. Other airlines are **LAN Colombia** ① *www.lan.com;* **Copa Airlines Colombia** ① *www.copaair.com;* **Satena** ① *www.satena.com*, government-owned but linked with Avianca on some flights; **EasyFly** ① *www.easyfly.com.co*, a budget airline serving Bogotá, Medellín, Cartagena and other smaller cities; **Viva Colombia** ① *www.vivacolombia.co*, a budget airline serving Barranquilla, Bogotá, Cartagena, Medellín, Montería, San Andrés and Santa Marta; and **Aerolínea de Antioquia (ADA)** ① *www.ada-aero. com*, based in Medellín, 19- to 32-seater planes serving most of the country. Domestic airports vary in the services they offer and tourist facilities tend to close early on weekdays, and all day Sunday. Local airport taxes are included in the price. Security checks can be thorough; watch your luggage.

A useful search engine for sourcing cheap flights is **www.despegar.com**. It may be worth using a travel agent to look for flights as they often have discount arrangements with certain airlines. You cannot buy tickets with an international credit card online, but you can pay over the phone. You can check online for good last-minute deals, as well as advance purchase fares.

Road

Almost all the main routes are paved, but the state of the roads, usually single-lane, varies considerably between departments. Journeys are generally comfortable, although heavy traffic can cause delays and landslides frequently close roads after heavy rain.

Bus

On the main routes, the bus network is comprehensive and buses are generally efficient. At large bus stations, the choice of carriers can be daunting but the advantage is that services are frequent. The scenery is worth seeing so travel by day if possible; it is also safer and you can keep a better eye on your valuables.

On main routes there is usually a choice of company and type of bus. The cheapest, *corriente*, are local buses, which are uncomfortable and slow, with frequent stops, but offer plenty of local colour. Try to keep your luggage with you. *Pullman* (each company has a different name for the service) are long-distance buses usually with air conditioning, toilets, hostess service and DVDs (almost always violent films, dubbed into Spanish). It's best to sit near the back where it's quieter and you don't have to keep the blinds down. The main companies operating in the region

> **Tip...**
> Throughout this guide, road names in addresses are shortened to 'C' meaning 'Calle' or Street; and 'Cra' meaning 'Carrera' or Avenue.

include: **Berlins del Fonce** ⓘ *www.berlinasdelfonce.com*, **Copetran** ⓘ *www.copetran.com.co*, and **Expreso Brasilia** ⓘ *www.expresobrasilia.com*. *Velotax* and other *busetas* are slightly quicker and more expensive than ordinary buses. They may be called *colectivos*, or *vans* and are usually 12- to 20-seat vehicles, sometimes seven-seater cars or pick-up trucks. It is also possible to order a *puerta-a-puerta* (door-to-door) service at a reasonable price. When taxis provide this service they are *porpuestos* (pay by seat) and do not leave till full. Fares shown in the text are no more than a guide. Note that meal stops can be few and far between, and short; it's best to take your own food. Luggage is normally carried in a locked compartment. **If you entrust your luggage to the bus companies' luggage rooms, remember to load it on to the bus yourself; it will not be done automatically.** There are few interdepartmental bus services on public holidays. During holidays and in high season, arrive at the bus terminal at least an hour before the departure time to guarantee a seat, even if you have bought a ticket in advance. If you are joining a bus at popular or holiday times, not at the starting point, you may be left behind even though you have a ticket and reservation. Always take your passport (or photocopy) with you: identity and luggage checks on buses do occur.

Car

With a good road network, self-driving is becoming an increasingly popular way of seeing Colombia. The kind of motoring you do will depend on the car you set out with. While a normal car will reach most places of interest, high ground clearance is useful for badly surfaced or unsurfaced roads and for fording rivers. Vehicles with 4WD are recommended for flexibility. Wherever you travel you should expect from time to time to find roads that are badly maintained, damaged or closed during the wet season; expect delays because of floods and landslides. There is also the possibility of delays due to major roadworks. Do not plan your schedule too tightly. There are *peajes* (toll stations) every 60-100 km or so on major roads: tolls depend on distance and type of vehicle, but vary from US$2-5.25. Motorcycles and bicycles don't have to pay.

Safety Before taking a long journey, ask locally about the state of the road and check if there are any safety issues. Roads are not always signposted. Avoid night journeys; the roads may not be in good condition, lorry and bus drivers tend to be reckless, and animals often stray onto the roads. Police and military checks can be frequent in troubled areas; keep your documents handy. In town, try to leave your car in an attended *parqueadero* (car park), especially at night. Only park in the street if there is someone on guard (tip US$0.50). Spare no ingenuity in making your car impenetrable. Your vehicle should be like an armoured van: anything less secure can be broken into by the determined and skilled thief. Be sure to note down key numbers and carry spares of the most important ones.

Documents International driving licences are advised, especially if you have your own car. To be accepted, a national driving licence must be accompanied by an official translation if the original is in a language other than Spanish. To bring a car into Colombia, you must also have documents proving ownership of the vehicle, and a tourist card/transit visa. These are normally valid for 90 days and must be applied for at the Colombian consulate in the country which you will be leaving. A *carnet de passages* is recommended when entering with a European registered vehicle. Only third-party insurance issued by a Colombian company is valid; there are agencies in all ports. You will frequently be asked for this document while driving. Carry driving documents with you at all times.

Fuel 'Corriente' 84 octane, US$5 per gallon. More expensive 'Premium 95' octane is only available in large cities. Diesel US$4.55.

Car hire Car hire, though relatively expensive, especially if you are going to the more remote areas and need 4WD or specialist vehicles, is convenient for touring, and the better hotels all have safe parking. The main international car rental companies are represented at principal airports but may be closed on Saturday afternoons and Sundays. There are also local firms in most of the departmental capitals. In addition to a passport and driver's licence, a credit card may be asked for as additional proof of identity and to secure a returnable deposit to cover any liability not covered by the insurance. If renting a Colombian car, note that major cities have the *pico y placa* system, www.picoyplaca.info, which means cars are not allowed to enter the city during morning and afternoon rush hour depending on the day and car number plate (this does not apply at weekends and on public holidays).

Essentials A-Z

Accident and emergency

General line for all emergencies: T123; Policía Nacional: T112; **Fire**: T119; **Red Cross emergency**: T132; **CAI Police**: T156. If you have problems with theft or other forms of crime, contact a **Centro de Atención Inmediata (CAI)** office for assistance. Make sure you obtain police/medical reports in order to file insurance claims.

Electricity

110 Volts AC, alternating at 60 cycles per second. Most sockets accept both continental European (round) and North American (flat) 2-pin plugs.

Embassies and consulates

For embassies and consulates of Colombia, see http://embassy.goabroad.com.

Festivals

End Jan **Hay Festival Cartagena**, www.hayfestival.com/cartagena. A branch of the UK's Hay Festival turns Cartagena into a focus for all things literary for 4 days.
End Jan/early Feb **Fiestas de Nuestra Señora de la Candelaria**. Celebrated in towns, including Cartagena, this religious cult festival was inherited from the Canary Islands, where 2 goat herders witnessed the apparition of the Virgin Mary holding a green candle.
Feb/Mar **Barranquilla Carnival** (movable), www.carnavaldebarranquilla.org. Beginning 4 days before Ash Wed, this is one of the best carnivals in South America. 4 days of partying are compulsory by law and involve parades and plenty of dancing.
End Feb or early Mar **Cartagena International Film Festival**, www.ficcifestival.com. One of South America's most important film festivals.
Mar/Apr **Semana Santa** (Holy Week) (movable). Celebrated all over Colombia, but the processions in Mompós are particularly revered.
26-30 Apr **Festival de la Leyenda Vallenata**, www.festivalvallenato.com. One of the most important music festivals in Colombia, 4 days of music making, celebrations and serious competition in Valledupar culminate in the selection of the best *vallenato* song and musicians in various categories.
1st 2 weeks of Nov **Independence of Cartagena and Concurso Nacional de la Belleza**. Cartagena celebrates being the first department to win Independence from the Spanish each 11 Nov with parades and traditional dancing in the streets. This has been somewhat supplanted by the National Beauty Pageant in which the winner will go on to represent Colombia at Miss Universe.

Public holidays
1 Jan **New Year's Day**
6 Jan **Epiphany***
19 Mar **St Joseph***
Easter **Maundy Thursday; Good Friday**
1 May **Labour Day**
May **Ascension Day*** (6 weeks and a day after Easter Sunday)

May/Jun **Corpus Christi*** (9 weeks and a day after Easter Sunday)
Jun **Sacred Heart*** (movable)
29 Jun **Saint Peter and Saint Paul***
20 Jul **Independence Day**
7 Aug **Battle of Boyacá**
15 Aug **Assumption***
12 Oct **Columbus' arrival in America*** (Día de la Raza)
1 Nov **All Saints' Day***
11 Nov **Independence of Cartagena***
8 Dec **Immaculate Conception**
25 Dec **Christmas Day**

When those marked with an asterisk (*) do not fall on a Mon, they will be moved to the following Mon. Public holidays are known as *puentes* (bridges).

Health

See your GP or travel clinic at least 6 weeks before departure for general advice on travel risks and vaccinations. Try phoning a specialist travel clinic if your own doctor is unfamiliar with health conditions in Colombia. Make sure you have sufficient medical travel insurance, get a dental check, know your own blood group and if you suffer a long-term condition such as diabetes or epilepsy, obtain a Medic Alert bracelet/necklace (www.medicalert.co.uk). If you wear glasses, take a copy of your prescription.

Vaccinations

It is advisable to vaccinate against polio, tetanus, diphtheria, typhoid, hepatitis A, and also rabies if going to more remote areas.

Health risks

The most common cause of travellers' **diarrhoea** is from eating contaminated food. In Colombia, drinking water is rarely the culprit, although it's best to be cautious (see below). Swimming in sea or river water that has been contaminated by sewage can also be a cause; ask locally if it is safe. Diarrhoea may also be caused by viruses, bacteria (such as E-coli), protozoal (such as giardia), salmonella and cholera. It may be accompanied by vomiting or by severe abdominal pain. Any kind of diarrhoea responds well to the replacement of water and salts. Sachets of rehydration salts can be bought in most chemists and can be dissolved in boiled water. If the symptoms persist, consult a doctor. **Tap water** in the major cities is in theory safe to drink but it may be advisable to err on the side of caution and drink only bottled or boiled water. Avoid having ice in drinks unless you trust that it is from a reliable source.

Mosquitoes are more of a nuisance than a serious hazard but some, of course, are carriers of serious diseases such as **malaria**, so it is sensible to avoid being bitten as much as possible. Sleep off the ground and use a mosquito net and some kind of insecticide. Mosquito coils release insecticide as they burn and are available in many shops, as are tablets of insecticide, which are placed on a heated mat plugged into a wall socket.

Money

US$1 = 2855 pesos; UK£1 =4189 pesos; €1=3307 pesos (May 2016).
Colombia's currency is the peso. New coins of 50, 100, 200, 500 and 1000 were introduced in 2012; as of 2016, the Banco de la República is issuing a new set of banknotes of 1000, 2000, 5000, 10,000, 20,000, 50,000 and, the newest denomination, 100,000 pesos. Larger banknotes can be hard to change,

especially in small towns, and in the morning. Watch out for forged notes. The 50,000-peso note should smudge colour if it is real; if not, refuse to accept it. There is a limit of US$10,000 on the import of foreign exchange in cash, with export limited to the equivalent of the amount brought in.

Exchange

Cash and traveller's cheques can in theory be exchanged in any bank, except the **Banco de la República**; go early to banks in smaller places to change these. In most sizeable towns there are *casas de cambio* (exchange shops), which are quicker to use than banks but sometimes charge higher commission. It's best to use euros and, even better, US dollars. It can be difficult to buy and sell large amounts of sterling. Hotels may give very poor rates of exchange. Hotels are not allowed to accept US$ as payment by law. Some may open a credit card account and give you cash on that. It is dangerous to change money on the streets and you may well be given counterfeit pesos, or robbed. Also in circulation are counterfeit US$ bills. You must present your original passport when changing money (it will be photocopied and you may be fingerprinted, too). Take some US$ cash with you for emergencies.

Credit/debit cards

It is unwise to carry large quantities of cash as credit cards are widely used, especially MasterCard and Visa; Diners Club is also accepted. American Express is only accepted in expensive places in Bogotá. Many banks accept Visa (Visaplus and ATH logos) and Cirrus/MasterCard (Maestro and Multicolor logos) to advance pesos against the card, or through ATMs. There are ATMs for Visa and MasterCard everywhere but you may have to try several machines. All **Exito** supermarkets have ATMs. ATMs do not retain cards – follow the instructions on screen. If your card is not given back immediately, do not proceed with the transaction and do not type in your pin number. There are reports of money being stolen from accounts when cards have been retained. ATMs dispense a frustratingly small amount of cash at a time. The maximum withdrawal is often 300,000 pesos (about US$100), which can accrue heavy bank charges over a period of time. For larger amounts try **Davivienda** (500,000 per visit) and **Bancolombia** (400,000 per visit).

Note Only use ATMs in supermarkets, malls or where a security guard is present. Don't ask a taxi driver to wait while you use an ATM. Be particularly vigilant around Christmas time when thieves may be on the prowl. Credit card loss or theft: Visa T01-800-912 5713; MasterCard T01-800-912 1303

Currency cards

If you don't want to carry lots of cash, prepaid currency cards allow you to preload money from your bank account, fixed at the day's exchange rate. They look like a credit or debit card and are issued by specialist money-changing companies, such as Travelex and Caxton FX. You can top up and check your balance by phone, online and sometimes by text.

Cost of living

Prices are a little lower than Europe and North America for services and locally produced items, but more expensive for imported and luxury goods. Modest, basic accommodation will cost about US$15-25 per person per night in Cartagena, Santa Marta and colonial cities, but a few dollars less elsewhere. A *menú ejecutivo* (set lunch) costs about US$3.50-5.50 and breakfast US$2-3. A la carte meals are usually good value too. Fierce competition for transport keeps prices low. Typical cost of internet is US$1-2 per hr.

Opening hours

Business hours depend a lot on where you are, so enquire locally. Most businesses such as banks and airline offices close for official holidays while supermarkets and street markets may stay open.

Banks Mon-Thu 0900-1500, 1530 on Fri.
Businesses Mon-Fri 0800-1700, but in hotter zones may close for lunch, 1200-1400, closing 1830 or 1900.
Shops Open 0700 or 0800 till 2000 and on Sat, but may close for lunch; supermarkets have longer hours and are open on Sat and Sun, usually 0900-1900.

Police and the law

You must carry identification at all times (see Visas, below). In the event of a vehicle accident in which anyone is injured, all drivers involved are usually detained until blame has been established, which may take several weeks. Never offer to bribe a police officer. If an official suggests that a bribe must be paid before you can proceed on your way, be patient and they may relent. In general, however, there are few hassles and most police are helpful to travellers.

Safety

The vast majority of Colombians are polite, honest and will go out of their way to help visitors and make them feel welcome. In general, anti-gringo sentiments are rare.

Drugs and scams

Colombia is part of a major drug-smuggling route. Police and customs' activities have greatly intensified and smugglers increasingly try to use innocent carriers. Do not carry packages for other people. Hotels are sometimes checked by the police for drugs. Make sure they do not remove any of your belongings. You do not need to show them any money. Cooperate but be firm about your rights.

There have been reports of travellers being victims of *burundanga*, a drug obtained from a white flower, native to Colombia. At present, the use of this drug appears to be confined to major cities. It is very nasty, almost impossible to see or smell. It leaves the victim helpless and at the will of the culprit. Usually, the victim is taken to ATMs to withdraw money. Be wary of accepting cigarettes, food and drink from strangers at sports events or on buses. In bars watch your drinks very carefully.

Other Colombian scams may involve fake police and taxicabs and there are variations in most major cities.

Guerrillas

Although greatly improved in recent years, the internal armed conflict in Colombia is almost impossible to predict and the security situation changes from day to day. For this reason, it is essential to consult regularly with locals for up-to-date information.

Taxi and bus drivers, local journalists, soldiers at checkpoints, hotel owners and Colombians who actually travel around their country are usually good sources of reliable information. Travelling overland between towns has in general become much safer due to increased military and police presence along main roads but it's best to avoid travelling at night. In some areas, however, fighting between the armed forces and guerrilla groups continues even though, at the time of writing, peace talks between both FARC and ELN and the government are taking place. For the purposes of this guide, only the area from **Urabá** near the border with **Panamá** into northwestern **Antioquia** and the border with Venezuela are considered *zonas calientes* (hot zones) where there may be significant unrest. Many other parts of the country are also regarded as *zonas calientes*, so if travelling beyond Cartagena and the Caribbean, make full enquiries when moving on. Hotels and hostels favoured by travellers are good places to ask.

Hotel security

The cheapest hotels are usually found near markets and bus stations but these are also the least safe and salubrious areas. Look for something a little better if you can afford it; if you must stay in a suspect area, try to return to your hotel before dark. If you trust your hotel, then you can leave any valuables you don't need in their safe-deposit box, but always keep an inventory of what you have deposited. An alternative to leaving valuables with the hotel administration is to lock everything in your pack and secure that in your room. Even in an apparently safe hotel, never leave valuable objects strewn about your room.

Theft

Pickpockets, bag snatchers and bag slashers are always a hazard for tourists, especially in crowded areas such as markets or the downtown cores of major cities. You should likewise avoid deserted areas, such as parks or plazas after hours. Be especially careful arriving at or leaving from bus stations. As a rule these are often the most dangerous areas of most towns and are obvious places to catch people carrying a lot of important belongings.

Leave unnecessary documents and valuables at home. Those you bring should be carried in a money-belt or pouch, including your passport, airline tickets, credit and debit cards. Hide your main cash supply in several different places. Never carry valuables in an ordinary pocket, purse or day-pack. Keep cameras in bags or day-packs and generally out of sight. Do not wear expensive wrist watches or jewellery. If you are wearing a shoulder-bag or day-pack in a crowd, carry it in front of you.

Women travellers

Unaccompanied foreign women may be objects of some curiosity. Don't be unduly scared – or flattered. Avoid arriving anywhere after dark. Remember that for a single woman a taxi at night can be as dangerous as wandering around alone. If you accept a social invitation, make sure that someone knows the address and the time you left. Ask if you can bring a friend (even if you do not). As elsewhere, watch your alcohol intake at parties with locals, especially if you are on your own. A good general rule is to always look confident and pretend you know where you are going, even if you do not. Don't tell strangers where you are staying.

Taxes

Airport taxes

The airport departure tax in most Colombian airports is about US$35, payable in dollars or pesos; see www. eldorado.aero. In Caribbean airports, however, the tax is higher: US$40 at Cartagena (see www.sacsa.co) and US$80 at Barranquilla. At Santa Marta the airport tax is now included in the ticket price (as of Feb 2016). Travellers changing planes in Colombia and leaving the same day are exempt from this tax. When you arrive, ensure that all necessary documentation bears a stamp for your date of arrival. There is also an airport tax on internal flights, about US$6 at Cartagena (US$5 at other airports), usually included in the ticket price.

VAT

16%. Ask for an official receipt if you want it documented. Some hotels and restaurants add *IVA* (VAT) onto bills. Strictly speaking foreigners should be exempt from this, but there seems to be some confusion about the application of this law. Raise the matter with your hotel and you may well get a discount. Some hotels add a small insurance charge.

Telephone *Country code T+57.*

Ringing: equal tones with long pauses. Engaged: short tones with short pauses. National and international calls can be made from public phone offices in all major cities and rural towns. You are assigned a cabin in which to make your calls; pay on the way out. You can also make calls from street vendors who hire out mobile phones (usually signposted 'minutos'). For call boxes, phone cards are the best option. It is relatively inexpensive to buy a pay-as-you-go SIM card for your mobile phone. Mobile phone numbers start with a 3-digit prefix beginning with 3.

Time

GMT -5 all year round.

Tourist information

National tourism is part of the **Ministry of Commerce, Industry and Tourism**, C 28, No 13A-15, Bogotá, www.mincit.gov.co, with its portal, **Procolombia**, at the same address, p 35-36, T560 0100, www.colombia.travel and www.procolombia.co/en. Departmental and city entities have their own offices responsible for tourist information; see the text for local details. These offices should be visited as early as possible for information on accommodation and transport, but also for details on areas that are dangerous to visit. Otherwise contact Colombia's representation overseas. See also Volunteering, page 132.

Useful websites

www.experienciacolombia.com A useful website in Spanish. **www.ideam.gov.co** Weather forecasts and climate information, in Spanish and English. **wp.presidencia.gov.co** The government website. You can also access: **www.gobiernoenlinea.gov.co**, in Spanish and English.

National parks and nature reserves

The **National Parks Service** is at the Ministerio del Medio Ambiente, Vivienda y Desarrollo Territorial (Ministry of the Environment, www.minambiente. gov.co), Ecotourism office, Cra 10, No 20-30, p 1, Bogotá, T01-353 2400, Mon-Fri 0830-1700, www.parquesnacionales. gov.co (which has a list of regional offices). Staff can provide information about facilities and accommodation, and have maps. Some parks and protected areas require permits to visit; check with the head office where these must be obtained before going to the park. Do not go directly to the parks themselves. Some prices vary according to high and low seasons. High season includes: weekends, Jun-Jul, Dec-Jan, public holidays and Semana Santa. **Aviatur** travel agency, Av 19, No 4-62, Bogotá, T1-587 5181, www.aviaturecoturismo.com, has the concession for accommodation in Tayrona (address given in text, not always efficient).

The **Asociación Red Colombiana de Reservas Naturales de la Sociedad Civil**, Cra 59, No 90-15, Bogotá, www.resnatur. org.co, is a network of privately owned nature reserves that works with local people to build a sustainable model of environmentally friendly tourism.

Conservation websites

www.colparques.net Organización Colparques.

www.humboldt.org.co Site of Institute Von Humboldt, probably the most important environment research organization in Colombia. An excellent site with descriptions of the different ecosystems in the country and projects with ethnic communities (in Spanish).

www.natura.org.co Fundación Natura, excellent conservation information.

www.proaves.org FundaciónProAves, an NGO dedicated to the study and conservation of birds and their habitats; publishes a good *Field Guide to the Birds of Colombia*.

Visas and immigration

To visit Colombia as a tourist, nationals of most Western countries do not need a visa. Tourists are allowed to stay a maximum of 180 days in a calendar year. Make sure that you are granted enough days for your visit. On entry you are given 90 days. If you wish to extend your permission to stay in Colombia, for a further 90 days, apply 2-3 days before your permit expires at a **Centro Facilitador de Servicios Migratorios (CFSM)** of **Migración Colombia** (www. migracioncolombia.gov.co gives a full list); it costs about US$33. Take 2 copies of your passport details, the original entry stamp, 2 passport photos and a copy of your ticket out of Colombia. This does not apply to visas (see below). If you overstay an entry permit or visa, a *salvoconducto* can be applied for at a CFSM. The *salvoconducto* is only issued once for a period of 30 days and is usually processed within 24 hrs; it costs about US$20. Take 2 recent photos and copies of your passport. The **Migración Colombia** head office in Bogotá is at C 26, No 59-51, Edif Argos Torre 3, p 4, T1-605 5454, www.migracioncolombia. gov.co. Arrive early in the morning, expect long queues and a painfully slow bureaucratic process.

Note Migración Colombia does not accept cash payments; these are made at the branches of Banco de Occidente with special payments slips (in Maicao, use **Banco de Bogotá**). An onward ticket may be asked for at land borders or Bogotá international airport. You may be asked to prove that you have sufficient funds for your stay.

When entering the country, you will be given the copy of your *DIAN* (Customs) luggage declaration. Keep it; you may be asked for it when you leave. If you receive an entry card when flying in and lose it while in Colombia, apply to any **Migración Colombia** office which should issue one and restamp your passport for free. Normally passports are scanned by a computer and no landing card is issued, but passports still must be stamped on entry. Note that to leave Colombia you must get an exit stamp from the Migración Colombia. They often do not have offices at the small border towns, so try to get your stamp in a main city.

Note It is highly recommended that you photocopy your passport details, including entry stamps which, for added insurance, you can have witnessed by a notary. Always carry a photocopy of your passport with you, as you may be asked for identification. This is a valid substitute for most purposes though not, for example, for cashing TCs or drawing cash across a bank counter. Generally acceptable for identification (eg to enter government buildings) is a driving licence, provided it is plastic, of credit card size and has a photograph. For more information, check with your consulate.

Tourist visa

Visas (issued only by Colombian consulates) are required by nationals of the Middle East (except Israel and UAE), Asian countries (except Japan, South Korea, Phillipines, Indonesia and Singapore), Cuba, Haiti, Nicaragua, Serbia, Bosnia and Herzegovina, Kosovo, Macedonia, Montenegro and all African countries (except South Africa). Always check for changes in regulations before leaving your home country.

Student and business visas

If you are going to take a Spanish course, you must have a student visa (US$50, plus US$15 charge), valid for 1 year. You may not study on a tourist visa. A student visa can be obtained while in Colombia on a tourist visa. Proof of sufficient funds is necessary. You must be first enrolled on a course from a bona fide university to apply for a student visa.

Various business visas and other temporary visas are needed for foreigners who reside in Colombia for longer than 180 days.

The **Ministerio de Relaciones Exteriores**, C 10, No 5-51, Bogotá, T381 4000, www.cancilleria.gov.co, Mon-Fri 0800-1230, 1330-1700, processes student and some work visas. In general, Colombian work visas can only be obtained outside Colombia at the appropriate consulate or embassy. You must register work and student visas at a **Migración Colombia** office within 15 days of obtaining them, otherwise you will be liable to pay a hefty fine. Visas must be used within 3 months. Supporting documentary requirements for visas change frequently. Check with the appropriate consulate in good time before your trip.

Volunteering

Foreigners over 18 can participate on the voluntary park ranger programme with the **National Parks Service**. Details are available from the **Ecotourism** office in Bogotá (see page 131), www.parques nacionales.gov.co. You will have to provide photocopies of ID documents and Colombian entry stamp in your passport. A good level of Spanish is required.

Weights and measures

Colombia uses the metric system, but US gallons for petrol.

Index

Entries in bold refer to maps

Credits

Footprint credits
Editor: Nicola Gibbs
Production and layout: Emma Bryers
Maps: Kevin Feeney
Colour section: Patrick Dawson

Publisher: Felicity Laughton
　　　　　　　Patrick Dawson
Marketing: Kirsty Holmes
Sales: Diane McEntee
Advertising and content partnerships:
Debbie Wylde

Photography credits
Front cover: Alice Nerr/shutterstock.com
Back cover top: Ildi Papp/Shutterstock.com
Back cover bottom: Anamaria Mejia/Shutterstock.com
Inside front cover: Fotos593/Shutterstock.com, Jess Kraft/Shutterstock.com, Martin Mecnarowski/Shutterstock.com.

Colour section
Page 1: Fotos593/Shutterstock.com.
Page 2: Fotos593/Shutterstock.com.
Page 4: meunierd/Shutterstock.com.
Page 5: Venturelli Luca/Shutterstock.com, Jess Kraft/Shutterstock.com, max blain/Shutterstock.com.
Page 6: Kobby Dagan/SuperStock.com.
Page 7: Ricard MC/Shutterstock.com, Jess Kraft/Shutterstock.com.
Page 8: Kobby Dagan/SuperStock.com.
Duotones
Page 24: Byron Aguilar/Shutterstock.com.
Page 50: Fotos593/Shutterstock.com.

Publishing information
Footprint Cartagena & Caribbean Colombia
3rd edition
© Footprint Handbooks Ltd
July 2016

ISBN: 978 1 910120 81 1
CIP DATA: A catalogue record for this book is available from the British Library

® Footprint Handbooks and the Footprint mark are a registered trademark of Footprint Handbooks Ltd

Published by Footprint
6 Riverside Court
Lower Bristol Road
Bath BA2 3DZ, UK
T +44 (0)1225 469141
F +44 (0)1225 469461
footprinttravelguides.com

Distributed in the USA by
National Book Network, Inc.

Printed in Spain by GraphyCems

Every effort has been made to ensure that the facts in this guidebook are accurate. However, travellers should still obtain advice from consulates, airlines, etc about travel and visa requirements before travelling. The authors and publishers cannot accept responsibility for any loss, injury or inconvenience however caused.